The Leadership Secret

-

The Ugly Truth

M A. GRANT

ISBN-10: 1511583711
ISBN-13: 978-1511583718

British Library Catalogue in Publication Data:
A catalogue record for this book is available from the British Library.

US Library of Congress Control Number:
LCCN: 2015907599

www.the-leadership-secret.com

DEDICATION

This book is dedicated to Tina, Olivia and Eva

CONTENTS

ACKNOWLEDGMENTS

From an early age I discovered the fascinating world of acknowledgments, since here was a way of getting closer to the writer and the artist. As I became an avid reader, my interest in acknowledgements grew, especially when I realized how difficult it is write a book of your own. There is something extremely difficult, even impossible, about naming everyone who has contributed to your work and to your personal development when you have been influenced by so many people, without at time even noticing their contribution or knowing they would have such a substantial impact.

I want to start by apologizing to anyone I may have omitted, I did not do so willingly or knowingly. There are some in particular who have given me license over the years to operate freely within their businesses in a way that has directly enriched this text.

My thanks and gratitude go out to you all.

Introduction

After twenty years in the field of leadership consulting it finally dawned on me that nearly everything that you may have read or have been shown about leadership, management, coaching and training would have been based on the overriding monumental success of others and/or the desire to make serious money – indeed, you only have to visit a bookshop or library to see row after row of books on the subject.

Each book would go on to explain how leadership works, and that by following a few simple rules, steps and procedures you will excel and gain truly amazing results within leadership. All this can be achieved by reading a couple chapters of a book? It can be over whelming to browse the business section looking for something that stands out as helpful or practical that isn't there purely to make money from you.

Looking back, could you probably remember a time when you were in your local book shop or library just browsing through books in the management or leadership section? Like me, I am sure you had the feeling that it all looked very complicated indeed. Reading the authors' suggestions on how all we had to do was follow a "twenty six step" programme to achieve complete leadership fulfilment. How did those authors come up with twenty six?

When, if ever, did you see them explain or state "and this is where I achieved the fulfilment of creating this program", or "here is the design process that I followed enabling this particular programme to achieve success", or even "here is the empirical evidence from this company that it worked successfully for." Where is the evidence of those things that didn't necessarily go to plan?

There must be development areas. They can't have created these amazing theories from scratch? They couldn't have all worked straight away? Surely it's not as simple as that, is it? If it was that easy we would all be doing it, wouldn't we? Where did they find an organization willing to test these twenty six steps? When do they tell you the truth on how they got there, and where is the chapter 'and this is what really happened?

Training workshops are the same, and I'm sure you may have attended a two day workshop that was delivered by an individual who had little training experience, or perhaps had been recruited by a training company straight from school. I have had this happen to me during several workshops which suggested that I would gain all the knowledge I would need to get the performance within any organization as long as I followed the guidelines, given that nothing goes wrong or would go wrong.

We will all have just sat there listening but not really believing. At least it would have been two days out of the office. What could you have really accomplished in two days? Usually on the these workshops there is seldom any contextualization of the subject that is being delivered linked to the working environment. If there is little contextualization, where is the Return On Investment (ROI).

I recently observed a project management programme that was delivered to an organization as part of an in-house programme where the trainer seemed confident and knowledgeable. When I looked deeper they were basing the programme around project managing the booking of a holiday, what was the point of that? What would be the ROI in the workplace? Surely they could have considered something that was more relevant to the particular company, something that would have enabled training transfer to take place. It was, after all, an in-house program, so there was no excuse.

The truth is that most of these short workshops and programs are designed with one thing in mind, making money! Not for you, but for them. Ask yourself this: if they were truly this knowledgeable and successful, then why are they delivering this workshop and not earning great sums of money in the real world? Ask yourself: when did these instructors, during or teaching these workshops, show you "and" this is what it looks like to coach, consult etc. in an organization? Or was it all role play? Where is the ROI, how do they ensure that this takes place?

Imagine you are on a twelve step programme on how to be a millionaire; you're sat there listening to the young facilitator explaining how you can become a millionaire by simply following these twelve steps. They seem dynamic and are full of the kind of the words that one would expect. They remind me of my experiences of used car salesmen, where they are using the sales pitch to get you to buy the car that you don't really want or need, but will give them the bonus on sales that they need.

They open the course and ask are there any questions – and I think to myself; yes, how much is in your bank account? Are you a millionaire? Where is the proof? Not from the money from this program, where is the proof from following these twelve steps? Then wait for the answer that the facilitator has been programmed to respond with. The answer is that these are facilitators that are just there to deliver a programme on behalf of a training organization and that is their employment, and this is why they struggle with the contextualization in the workplace.

Of course there are trainers are able to contextualise and have been successful, this is their way of giving back? But normally it is about making money, especially if it is a programme delivered by a external training company that is based on profit. The trainers and facilitators that do demonstrate this are the exception rather than the rule – or are they? Are there a large number of these trainers that do have the right kind of value set? Do they have the right beliefs that allow them the behaviour that set them apart? This is something that will be looked at throughout this book.

Most of these training companies use outsourced trainers that are not working for the training company, in which case they are even less likely to be qualified or experienced within this field. They are only delivering the programme as a source of income. These training companies spend a lot of time and resources on securing business; they are able to strike a sound level of rapport with companies only for all the hard work to be undone by outsourcing the instructor. This is common practice amongst external training companies.

This book is about my journey as a consultant in the field of leadership, it's about discovering how I went on to become a leadership Subject Matter Expert (SME), and becoming truly effective at getting organizations to achieve the results they really wanted through leadership development. It was about discovering the journey that would enable my behaviour to change, and in this context it's about leadership, coaching, management, training, and about finding a term to call myself in a congested field of leadership. This would allow individuals and organizations to get the performance that they wanted, and, more importantly, that they needed.

This is not a about my success, but about going through life and getting what you want through learning from mistakes, mishaps and successes. In this book I will share some of the amazing stories of success and some amazing stories of failure. That is right, failure, and there have been occasions when it has gone spectacularly wrong, and I have had to get it wrong to learn. I can't have been the all-round Leader straight from the off, can I?

If we were looking at coaching as an example, this would be what a life coach may be expected to say – "Martin, that's great, and you have just spoken about failure, but really there is no failure there is only feedback." It is easy to understand that from a coaching perspective, but how do you tell the CEO of the company that there is no failure, there is only feedback, when the results of performance haven't matched expectations and they are now having to look at laying off members of staff? This is the real world, where it's all about the bottom line.

These are experiences of my proven coaching, leadership, management, and any other experiences that have worked in the workplace to ensure performance. This is a journey of leadership from humble beginnings to being able to deliver at the highest level of leadership to some of the largest companies in industry. The chapters on Leadership and Coaching also act as the technical aspect of the book, so if you're looking for the technical knowledge and theories they are covered within those chapters.

For diehard enthusiasts the references at the back of this book are the books, articles and journals that I think have made real impact or provide a useful read to enhance personal knowledge. The references also go on to form a detailed reading list that explains some of the current thinking on leadership.

How does one go on to become a leadership consultant?

Are you just born with the skill sets to get the best out of people and organizations? Do we automatically know how to improve the bottom line and how to get a Return On Investment (ROI)? Do you know how to lead or show others how to lead? There are individuals who do have this natural ability, what is their secret? Here, in this context, "we" are with the rest of us, those that have to learn how to do it.

Within this book I am going to share with you the answers to these questions above and more, I am going to show you the secret to leadership. Like all great leadership secrets, it starts in the beginning...

M A. Grant

Chapter 1

In the Beginning...

It's always the difficult part; where do you start? How could I explain the leadership secret from a starting point? We could go back to the beginning, whilst I was at school, but that perhaps that's too far back, for the real leadership secret begins within my early career development.

I was sunning myself in Sierra Leone in 2006, delivering some of the best leadership consultancy, that I thought at the time on behalf of the Department for International Development (DIFD). This was as a part of the United Kingdom's (UK) plan to help prepare the country for its first free elections after the now infamous civil war.

I received a phone call from my then UK employer at the

time, who then went on to explain, "Great news, Martin, you have done an amazing job and you are to be rewarded with a top job helping with the set-up of a Leadership Training School for members of the UK Government. The main focus will be on leadership and coaching for performance within government organizations that are struggling with performance targets."

Afterwards I thought, how hard could that be, as I had already been working as what I thought to be a reasonably competent consultant within the world of leadership, coaching, management and training. I had gone through an extensive development programme that had seen me work on numerous projects for various Government bodies within the UK that now had me positioned at the top within the consulting world – or so I had thought.

Initial Career Development

Prior to the role in Sierra Leone I had joined the UK Government as a young naive individual with no real formal education, wearing blinkers to the world and how it operated. I had progressed at a steady rate, gaining a couple of early promotions along the way; these were more luck than ability, being in the right place and at the right time. I then made a life changing decision to go on and train as a trainer as part of a Government scheme to get employees involved in training.

They invested a lot of time, resources and money towards developing me during a period of six months extensive training in which leadership skills were imparted to me, which led me to become a top notch consultant, trainer, facilitator and all round great guy! I had travelled the world delivering my knowledge and extensive skill set to others, and the results were truly awe inspiring, or so I thought.

Of course that is not entirely true. What had happened was that I was trained to deliver consultancy, coaching and training, however, the delivery method was very much a case of do as I say. It suggested that if you follow what I have been telling you then you would get results. The training at this time was autocratic. I remember an instance when another student had started to deliver his instruction and he made the mistake of putting his hand in their pocket.

The lesson that they had delivered was one of the best instructional periods I had seen at that time, however, the major point that the instructor picked up on whilst delivering their feedback was structured around the student having their hand in their pocket. I remember thinking that the trainer had in three minutes of feedback destroyed all the clear potential that this individual had. They never went on to reproduce that level of instruction again, but on the other hand they never put their hand in their pocket either.

The trainer that was conducting the instruction appeared to have never taught to real students, only individuals who were becoming trainers, and therefore he had little credible experience to fall back on; it was very much a case of theoretical facilitation. Certainly they did not provide any real life experiences of what to expect in real terms, but it was conducted with clinical delivery. The delivery though was of the highest order, and you be hard pushed to find better individuals able to deliver this training function in other large organizations, as long as individual's hands were out of their pockets.

After successful completion of this training I was then tasked to deliver this knowledge myself to unsuspecting potential trainers, and to believe that I was this font of all knowledge. I would at the time explain to my students that they were lucky to be receiving this training from me. Certainly in those days I had the ego the size of Manchester United Football Club, but found myself in that position of training with little experience to fall back, on just like the instructor before me.

At this time we were telling students that we were here to teach them methods, and impart those different methods to achieve the respective instructional aims that the students would be assessed on. This assessment would form part of the feedback on the students ability to instruct. Subject matter was not that important as long as the methods adopted were workable.

A group of instructors, including myself, were having coffee when a heated argument broke out over methods and that there is always a right method that is the best way, and if it's not adopted then the students should be marked down accordingly. Imagine the effect that this could have on you if you were the student? Marked down for employing a method that although workable didn't agree with the instructors' chosen methods.

Certainly for myself, I would mark according to whether the method was workable or not. For some of the instructors, if it wasn't their favourite method that was adopted then they would mark the student down, even if the method had been workable.

The approach of "we were here to teach methods" had gone in a thirty second exchange, and resulted in a speedy regression to do as I say not as I do. A complete regression into transactional behaviour. This was one of the first instances that I experienced where sometimes the values of the individuals were in conflict of that of the organization ,which resulted in the negative behaviour of some the instructors. That saying of "in times of stress, people regress" was certainly evident.

I have often thought of this moment, as at the time alarm bells were ringing. I wasn't aware of the significance, but knew it was important, along with the hand in the pockets, a reminder that sometimes we lose track of what is happening in front of us and how easy it is to regress. I would later go on to use this as an example when explaining behaviour, and how easy it is to regress, particularly when associated with stress, as a detailed case study in behavioural change.

After a period of time spent imparting this initial training I was then let loose on unsuspecting CEO's within certain government organizations, who were told that I was the font of all knowledge, a SME. These organizations would look to me to provide the consultancy piece on their respective training. I had never done this for real but I had the classroom know-how and the persona of a second hand car sales-man. Which was fortunate at the time as there was no formal training beforehand. I was very much selling myself to the fact that I knew what I was talking about, and that they would be fools to ignore any advice that I was giving them as I was the expert consultant within the field or discipline of training.

This was not conventional selling as in a product, but I was selling myself. In fact there was a product, the product was me. Faced with the CEOs, it was a case of thinking on my feet and doing the best to convince them that I knew what I was talking about, as at times there was a certain amount of "bluffing" going on. This bluffing was me selling this to the unsuspecting CEOs, who took my knowledge as granted. If they were to really have scratched beneath the surface they would notice that there was no depth to what I was saying. In fact there was little depth in me.

I had realized very quickly that if I kept things very simple and easy to follow that results would happen, and the reason for this simplicity was my lack of in-depth knowledge. If the organization had started to get results it made me look good at the same time. With this swift promotion it resulted in me gaining success, which in turn led me to providing a higher level of consultancy and giving strategic direction where applicable. The reason that I had to keep it simple was due to my real lack of experience and knowledge.

I was trained in leadership, and although I had been taught some great coaching it was still a case of being very transactional in its delivery. Certainly I would ask effective questions, but I wasn't listening, I already had the answers that I was going to use or ensure that they use. The effective questions that I was asking had come from a bank of questions that I had used in the past, but because I had already got the solution I was merely going through the motions. There was no real substance to them.

What I had been doing in essence was getting away with it. If someone were to have looked closely at my performance I would easily have been be caught out. I had been allowed to get away with it. The scary thing is that I was not alone in this; all my peers except for the odd exception were doing the same because they too had this lack of experience and knowledge.

It is interesting to look back at those of my peers who were the odd exception to this and to look at the results that they were getting. Looking back, it would have been interesting to see how they got those results? To role model their behaviour and actions so that others could have got similar results using their behaviours and actions.

The Anti-Coach

It happens to us all at some stage, the blocker, the anti person, the barrier, the one individual who gets in the way. This is not just in a business sense or work environment, but also from a personal perspective too. They become the thorn in your side, always showing up when you really don't want them too. Or they have that ability to turn a good idea into the worst idea. For some reason they are always there, whether it be at school, later in work and in our personal life. You know the person I am talking about, for me it is was a case of them ending up my arch nemesis at that particular time.

My first experience of how this affected me as a consultant happened during this initial training development stage of my career. The individual[1] in question had all the natural ability as an instructor, trainer and consultant that I wished I had at that time. Indeed, if you were to put in a box what a trainer should look like it would have been the Anti-Coach. You could place them in a box and put a sign on it explaining "break in case of trainer and/or consultant as required", similar to a fire alarm that says "break in case of emergency."

However, with this natural ability came a natural arrogance, a way of influencing others to get results and decisions that weren't necessary the right one for the individuals but were right for the Anti-Coach. If any other trainer had an opinion - unless it fitted in with the Anti-Coaches - it wasn't right.

The Anti-Coach had the line managers eating out of the palm of his hand too, they could do no wrong. He was the cultural architect within that specific time and place. Imagine a football team with an appointed captain, although for the appointed captain it doesn't mean that they are really in charge. Normally there is a cultural architect that the others will look to, or that they can control. Great if it is the captain, not so good if it's not. Take David Beckham when he played for England; not the captain, but he was the cultural architect, and as a result they achieved some credible performances when he played.

Now imagine that he was having a negative effect, he is still the cultural architect but now the team would be

---

[1] A follow up for this individual is covered in Chapter 8.

experiencing negative results. This is what was happening with me at the time with the Anti-Coach. The Anti-Coach was having a negative effect on me which in turn was affecting my performance.

At the time I wasn't aware of this or equipped to deal with this type of person, but it became for a while at the time, all consuming, why does this person get away with this? Why do they allow this to happen? It did start to affect my performance as I was now concerned with this person and not myself. The frustration of me seeing this, whilst others were not able to see what was going on, was a really intense feeling of frustration. The questions were: how could I get others to see what the Anti-Coach was doing? How could I get them to see the impact that this is having on other instructors and students alike?

In hindsight, I had been asking the wrong questions. Here was an individual who had all the skill sets, the natural ability, and was proven to get results, just not the values and behaviours to go with it. What could be done to change their values and beliefs? If this could be done, what would be the potential and performance from the Anti-Coach? What would be the consequences if the Anti-Coach couldn't change? What would be the effect long term for the organization with this type of toxic individual? What would be the affect on the Anti-Coach themselves? Surely they need to be considered too?

Sierra Leone

This was the pinnacle of my consultancy at the time, consulting on behalf of Department for International

Development (DFID) on all training matters in preparation to the first free elections post civil war.

I had a small team of United Kingdom (UK) consultants to assist with this task and we were employed to impart our knowledge and skills in leadership and training, and they would get all the results we were used to achieving. I was in my element and I was going to reap the rewards. Well, that was the thought process anyway.

What we were doing in fact was trying to force upon them a training methodology that had worked in some parts of the UK, however we were not flexible in adapting it to their needs. We were very much adopting a transactional approach and using a real sense of directive leadership in getting the up-take.

When things were not going our way we would resort to the "just get on and do it approach." Sure, we had similar experiences when we had been working with our respective workforce in the UK, and they just don't get it, there is that glazed look on the face of the individual, and we have to resort to the just get on with it! This was very much us regressing to the leadership style that we felt most comfortable with at the time. The one we normally adopted in times of stress was the old favourite transactional style.

Performance was measured using pass rates on courses that we had delivered, but we had flexibility to alter the pass rates and therefore we could fudge the figures, because of the numbers of individuals and the selection process pass rates were almost secured. What we were doing was cooking the books. It was easy to cook the books when you own the kitchen and the diners are your staff too.

The term cooking the books has always fascinated me, it's that clash of the internal moral compass, there is a reason why we need to cook them, but we know that cooking them is going to spoil something eventually. From a cooking perspective, when you cook the books you are normally creating false accounting. Why do we have to cook the books? surely if we are really that great as consultants, as coaches, we would come up with another way to get the results without having to step into the kitchen, we would all have a detailed recipe book.

This is where some of the leadership books will tell you that you need to have that detailed recipe book. Great in theory, but in reality something else. But this is what was happening at the time, and as I said we were getting results. We were getting these results by adopting a very transactional style of leadership by adapting the punishment and reward method, the carrot and stick.

So there I was, having sunned myself, I then received the phone call that would have the biggest impact on my career, it would go on to change everything.

The Phone Call

I received the phone call, "Great news, Martin, you have done an amazing job and you are to be rewarded with top job helping on the set up of a Leadership Training School for members of the UK Government. With the main focus on Leadership for performance within government organizations that were looking to increase their return on investment." The phone call was out of the blue, and the role was not what I had been expecting. I had been anticipating a role at the earlier establishment that I had started within, a role of senior training management. This new job was something that I had not expected, it had the words "leadership" and "school" in it. I had never heard of a leadership school before. What was a leadership school?

I started to ask questions; so what does this role entail? I received the following brief: "There have been a number of enquires at government level[2] into training and leadership, it was found that although training was happening, there was no training transfer. It also found that leadership was strong in transactional leadership, but transformational was not so well understood and in particular coaching was the least understood." As I sat there listening, one of the things that that had struck a chord was that they were suggesting, coaching as a leadership style.

They went on to say "that a study had been commissioned to look at Coaching, and it suggested when used effectively can support (Hardy *et el*, 2006) and develop trainers and coachees alike. But it was a theoretical piece, and no empirical evidence had been proven that it worked." I thought "no problem", it sounded like a case of cooking the books again to get the results which I had already a proven to be a competent chef.

---

[2] House of Commons Defence Committee (**HCDC**) and the Adult Learning Inspectorate (**ALI**) (DHALI) reports.

The UK Government were going to create a leadership school from scratch and design the coaching and leadership that would be adopted. This would include the design, strategic policy, training, and consultancy to name but a few. I would be acting as the lead consultant on this as a SME in leadership concentrating on coaching as an area of development.

When this was explained to me it all sounded very formal and there were individuals in authority that were taking it very seriously. I had noticed that there was money being allocated for development of this leadership school, which was odd as at the time the UK was in a time of recession, and investing money in development was not widely seen or common place.

It would also involve going out to industry and acting as the business coach/consultant and to measure the impact on performance through the changes that would be adopted as a result of the project.

After the Call

After the call I sat there in my office doing circles on an office swivel chair, thinking that after ten years of training and consultancy what could anyone have shown or taught me about leadership? What was there for me to learn? This was going to be an absolute doddle. I was going to turn up, cut and paste from somewhere else, and take all the credit for the impact and the results that would obviously happen as it was all common sense, wasn't it? I thought I knew everything…

Chapter 2 – The Leadership School

The School

I arrived at the leadership school, with the staff employed. Initially I thought that I would have had input into the recruiting of staff, but I arrived knowing that the individuals who I would be responsible for had already been recruited. I was surprised at how friendly everyone was and that the work environment was of a friendly nature. Normally the experience, when moving within the UK Government, has an air of doom and gloom, with individuals just coming to work like zombies.

The leadership school looked like it had been designed to create an atmosphere of positivity. Certainly from an organizational perspective, the emphasis was on the customer experience, and the customer in this instance consisted of the students attending the courses at the leadership school. This was really important to them at the school, and examples of this was that answering the phone in the right manner to the way voice mail was set up had carefully been thought about.

I was pleasantly surprised to see that the leadership school was different, there was a genuine "buzz." I was informed that the design of the school had incorporated the best learning technology to produce the best available learning environment for students attending courses. It had been fitted with the latest in educational technology, including an accommodation building for those learners requiring overnight facilities. A canteen that would rival quality restaurants, all at subsided prices, had been constructed. This had all been produced for the learners.

This was my first eye opener that it had been designed to enhance the performance of the learner, and it seemed that it is all about them. It was about taking the learners that came through the door or attended the school and allowing them to fulfil their respective potential.

The School had been set up as result of shortcomings in trainer performance across government which led to a train the trainer (TTT) programme being designed. This TTT programme was designed for the trainers and instructors who had already completed a trainer programme to ensure that there was a common base line for them.

The main goal of the TTT was to enhance their leadership, coaching and basic instructional skills and show them how to get a performance out of the learners within these core goals, it was about releasing potential. Each TTT course could cater for over 160 students and run with over 12 instructors delivering to the students. They were to be training over 2000 students a year; this for me was important as the objective was to train over 2000 students; it was a large operation that would have an impact across government behaviour and performance.

Organizational Change

Within the leadership school there were discussions around organizational change. I completed some investigation into organizational change and discovered that the ability of most organizations to respond to change, meanwhile, tends to be much slower than the world around them. The bigger the organization is, typically, the slower they are to respond. This had been the case in most of my previous roles, which invariably resulted in a relative drop in performance, which most organizations attempt to resolve with training.

How many times have you seen that in order to fix a shortfall in organizational performance you must increase the amount of training? The problem, however, is that this type of training is usually knowledge and skills based and invariably takes considerable time to deliver. Hence, by the time people have been trained, the organization has already changed and the training is now out of date. Furthermore, whilst performance might well be knowledge and skills based, it is ultimately people driven, such that the stress associated with both learning and coping with the change can be a problem in itself. This was interesting, as the school was the creating the conditions for a learning culture or the learning organization to take place.

It wasn't until the early 1980s that organizations had started to consider the concept of learning. Before this time, traditional state education, supported by up-front vocational training and strict management, was sufficient to sustain workplace performance and productivity in a relatively unchanging world. There had to be a change, surely, because if individuals kept doing what they were doing they would keep getting the same results.

As a result, schools had embraced the concept of the learning organization, and now it has become the recognized blueprint of how organizations will have to behave in the future; not only to thrive, but in order to survive. This was recently evident during the global economic downturn.

It dawned on me at the time that the leadership school was going to be bigger than I had anticipated. I had started to grasp the size and role that the school was going to have on instruction across Government

The staff at the leadership school had been using strange language like releasing potential, developing individuals, action planning, goal setting, SMART[3] objectives – I remember thinking: what was this strange place I had walked into? Recently my daughter had been sitting on the couch with one of her friends, both were frantically texting away. I asked her, "Who are you two speaking to?" to

---

[3] For more information on SMART turn to chapter 4, which focuses on coaching.

which she replied, "Each Other!" This type of communication change is happening at a rapidly growing rate as technology moves forward. Imagine what would happen if you lost your smart phone for two days, what would be the impact on you?

I had started to feel that I was missing something and I needed to catch up on what was going on at the leadership school.

The Leadership Schools' Management Team

One of the interesting things I had noticed about the school was the management team; it was made up of individuals that had been drafted in to form the engine of the school. Unlike myself, who had been a dedicated training consultant, these were individuals that did not necessarily come from a training background. The CEO was one such individual, he had had a long career in management but not in training.

On one of my first days at the school I was informed that the CEO would be delivering a leadership lecture to a course currently on a TTT and I had decided that I would slip in the back of the lecture to watch what I thought would be a typical 'death' by PowerPoint lecture. I could not have been more wrong.

Here was the CEO delivering a Leadership lecture to a large group of young instructors who really should have, in my experience, been nodding off at this stage. What I saw was this individual, the CEO, having no formal training background, captivating the students; it was interactive and formative and one of the best presentations I had seen.

What made it all the more remarkable was my perception of Leadership had been completely "smashed." All of the previous Leadership lectures, training and programs that I had attended had been very much of how I regarded school; boring, with no charisma, sending me to sleep. The leadership that was being presented by the CEO was also different, it was something new. I had to find out more about this leadership and what made it so different.

I set out to discuss with the CEO why they had been delivering this on the TTT and not one of the instructors. The CEO explained that this was one of the most important subjects and that as the CEO they should be setting the example to all who come through the leadership school, including students and staff alike. That the CEO should lead from the front, demonstrating that this form of leadership is all encompassing, not exclusive for the top management, and that everyone has a role to play within it.

I asked the CEO about their performance as a lecturer and what was their formal training, and the CEO replied that he had attended a one day programme that hadn't really taught them anything. The CEO had decided that in order to achieve, his goals within the lecture he had to produce an action plan, and had been working to achieve the goals, and as they developed, his presentation skill set had also improved.

The CEO pointed out, that it wasn't a performance either, he wasn't there to perform as an actor, but to develop and release the potential of the learners. This was a really interesting use of language that was being used. When the CEO was delivering the lecture, he wasn't there to perform, and interestingly he also had his hands in his pockets throughout the delivery. If the Anti-Coach had of watched this, he would have not been impressed.

What really stood out was the CEO's sheer enthusiasm for the subject. It was also evident that he had passed on this enthusiasm to all of the attendees of that specific lecture.

The leadership school had also employed an education consultant, who was there to ensure that the best learning styles, educational means, subject matter and methods were employed. The consultant was to work alongside myself. This, for me at the time, was a bit of clash. Why did they need this person when they had me? After all, I had been training people for years and I was at the top. I had come across individuals like this in the past and we had never got on. I had decided that we were not going to get along.

Interestingly the first time that I sat down with him to discuss our roles. I was expecting to have this huge clash of egos, as we were employed in similar roles. In the space of five minutes all of my preconceived feelings and perceptions dissolved. I found him to be a really refreshing individual, with modern outlook on life. We had a long conversation about training instructors, and what he was saying was exactly the same as what I had been used to.

I had thought this was great, we are using the same language, but the more that we talked the more I realised that I had been training individuals to be instructors using the correct methods, which was reassuring, but I had no underpinning knowledge of where these methods came from, how and why were they designed?

This individual educational consultant that I had thought initially I would immensely dislike had all of the underpinning knowledge that I did not. I found myself wanting to know more, they had sparked something inside me, and it was as if they had lit a tiny ember that would go on to fuel my own personal quest for knowledge.

I owe a lot to this individual, and to the subsequent conversations that we would go on to have. It's often interesting that those individuals we may perceive as a threat go on to have a deep and meaningful relationship with. However, that's not to confuse them with someone like the Anti-Coach.

I had realised that although I had been "acting" as a consultant for some time I only had this surface knowledge, I had no underpinning, no depth to support what I was consulting on, although I was correct I couldn't tell anyone why I was correct, I couldn't provide any supporting knowledge.

The Leadership School's Trainers

It was important that I meet the instructors at the school, so I decided that I would take some time to watch them in action and get a feel for their standard. This was something that I had done in the past, that would enable me to then give the trainers improvement tips, and advice on how to improve and develop as trainers; this is what I had done throughout my initial career.

Normally when I had gone to watch another instructor I could see the fear in their face, that perception that I'm here to destroy them and their instructional ability, to tell them exactly what they should have done or what I would have done. This relates to that style of instruction that I had employed earlier.

I was sitting at the back of the classroom for the instruction from the first instructor that I had decided I would watch, and he was delivering to a group of 12 from the TTT, and it was delivered with the same vigour and enthusiasm that the CEO has used in the leadership lecture. Certainly he had their hands in their pockets, and some of the professionalism that I would normally expect was all over the place, but the students were engrossed and fully active and participative in the period of instruction.

At the end of the presentation the instructor asked me to stay behind and give him feedback; this was so that they could improve future lessons. It was strange, as normally instructors loath the type of feedback that I would give.

I asked the instructor about this feedback and he said that they had this feedback system that was used; the instructor said that they would be using it later that day on one of the students from the TTT who had a performance task as part of the course. I explained to the instructor that I was really happy with what I had seen and that I would give formal feedback once I had found my feet at the school, but would come along to watch the student performance task. This was a really interesting development for me, an instructor requesting me to come back and observe more.

The student from the TTT had prepared a teaching practice that he would be delivering to other students from the TTT, and the instructor was going to watch and then give feedback on the period. I had explained to the instructor that I would only be observing and wouldn't get involved in their feedback.

We both then settled in to watch the student. As the student delivered his teaching practice, I made notes that I would have used to give the feedback, as if it was delivering the feedback. This way I could compare the instructor in relation to the points that they delivered to the student to those that I had noticed.

At the end of the period the instructor stood up and then proceeded to deliver his feedback. What was fascinating was the way he conducted the feedback session; all the points that I had written down were covered, but done in a different style. I asked them where they had leant how to do this.

They explained that the school had an external consultant who taught all the staff the methods, coaching feedback etc. to be adopted on the TTT. A common theme that I had picked up on was the term 'coaching.' The instructor went on to explain that by coaching the feedback out of the learner they were more likely to take responsibility for their future performance. Wait a minute, that should have been me saying that!

What was the difference in the attitude of the instructors at the leadership school? I noticed that this concept of the learning organization suggested the need for trainers that can help people learn, not so much what to learn but how to learn; and managers that can help people develop their emotional intelligence (EQ) alongside their technical competence and embrace the age-old skills of coaching. Here then was a strange concept, your EQ. I had heard of Intelligence Quotient (IQ), but what was this EQ? Again something that I would go on to have to look at.

I had noticed that coaching seemed to be a participative style of communication based on asking rather than telling. Coaching is recognized as a suggested way to truly empower people to take responsibility – for both their learning and their performance. Something at the time I had said I did, but only played lip service to, it had been only words for me. For the instructors it was now a behaviour that they placed value on.

The External Consultant

Having spoken to several of the instructors at the leadership school I decided to set up an meeting with the external consultant. I wasn't sure what to expect, since normally individuals or organizations had come to me for the consultancy and now I was going to be speaking to an external one myself. Straight away, all of my defences were raised, it was me that had all of the barriers and I was not going to like this person at all.

It turned out that my perception was way off, and the consultant was not what I was expecting at all. They had come from a similar background to me and had developed their knowledge over a long period. They had a really infectious likeability that got me to like them straight away. Later I discover that this was them using rapport building to great effect.

One of the roles that I was responsible for at the leadership school was to be develop a series of coaching programs in order to support the TTT and I needed the consultancy from them for this, again at the time the word 'coaching.' The consultant explained to me that although the TTT had coaching built into the programme to develop the students as coaches it was important to consider the training transfer and who was going to ensure that the coaches (students) are coaching when they got back to their respective companies.

I was beginning to ask questions: what do they mean by training transfer? The consultant asked, "How many times have I been on a course?" I give the sarcastic. "I have been on too many to mention" reply. The consultant then went on to explain that the real magic from a training point of view happens in the workplace.

The leadership school could teach the students everything that they needed in order to be the best that they can be, but how does the leadership school know that when they the students go to the workplace that they are using the new knowledge and skills? What the leadership school needed to do was ensure that the transfer of that knowledge into the workplace takes place. "How do we do that?" I asked the consultant.

The consultant went on to explain that instead of them telling me, why didn't I attend one of the coaching programs and discover for myself what this 'coaching' was about. This would be a great way to get to know the consultant. With that feeling of 'there is nothing new that they could show me' I had booked myself onto the next available course.

The Penny Drop

I had arrived on the coaching course that the consultant was delivering, with all the bravado of an experienced trainer/consultant and that I was not going to learn anything new. I was fascinated that there was music playing as I walked into the classroom, something that the consultant used to anchor specific training to, I only found out what anchoring[4] was later and its importance within training.

The consultant then proceeded to deliver the course. I found that as the course moved along, the coaching that the consultant was talking about was that I had been conducting throughout my career, but the "how to get there" and the terminology was different. The language that was used has meanings to, with a lot of emphasis placed on it.

The course was all about coaching and mentoring, but the consultant spent a long time positioning it within the leadership model that the students on the course could use back at their respective place of work. The leadership model that the students would use is explained in the next chapter. There was also time spent on the values and beliefs and how this affects our behaviour. Why would this be important in getting results? What has leadership got to do with results?

---

[4] Covered within the coaching chapter.

It then hit me: if we could get someone to take responsibility for their own performance by them placing a value on it through using leadership to guide them, then they would be more likely to get the desired result. You would still get a result but it would not be as good. What in fact you would be getting is a behavioural change.

I discovered that this outcome was part of the course and instead of telling me this I was allowed to discover it for myself, and speaking to the consultant at the end of the programme they went on to explain that this was one of the outcomes of the program. What I had now got by attending the programme was that behavioural change within me. I had taken my first steps in taking responsibility for my own actions, the penny had just dropped.

Academic Journey

Having returned from the coaching course my brain was in overdrive. I started researching all I that I could on leadership and coaching. I was trying to develop my own knowledge. What I discovered was that there were numerous academic pieces on leadership but few on coaching, and that it seemed that if you wanted credibility you needed post-nominal letters or post-nominal initials or post-nominal titles, or designator letters after your name.

What I needed at that time was advice on the best way to get post-nominal letters or post-nominal initials or post-nominal titles, or designator letters after my name, and of course the leadership school had its own education consultant, and I quizzed them on the fastest way to gain them after my name.

What I got was the education spin, that it was not about the initials or qualification, it's about the journey and the learning. I laughed, and said, "We are going to disagree" as for me it was about the quickest and easiest way to get them, this was an example of my current value system at this time.

I started to research all the universities in the UK, looking for a suitable academic programme that I could undertake that would give me the post nominal's as quickly as possible. I discovered a Masters Degree in leadership conducted at a respected UK university that used your career experience to reduce the time needed.

I was pleased to find out that using this Approved Prior Education Learning (APEL) I could get myself on to the last element of the academic program, the dissertation. Which meant I could do the programme in under a year, just what I felt was right for me, as quick as possible, taking the shortest route but still getting the desired results.

I attended the two day induction for the academic programme having decided that I was going to base all my research in the field of leadership and coaching that the leadership school was undertaking at the time. This I thought would be easy as all I was going to have to do was to write up my day job.

After the two day induction we were pretty much left to our own as this was the final part the dissertation. It dawned on me that I had never written a piece of academic work since school, certainly not at the Master's level. I had that feeling that at this level, more would be expected. I discovered that maybe in hindsight I should have done the first two years in preparation for the Master's.

The dissertation took over my life during evenings and weekends and the amount of time I had to dedicate to it was very much underestimated.

Half way through the dissertation a strange feeling had started to develop, and that was discovering that I had become less interested in the post nominal' letters, and more concerned with the academic journey. I was developing this feeling, and I found that once this was the case the journey was much more enjoyable. I can still hear the echo of the Education Consultant: "It's about the learning!"

I remember the feeling of a job well done as it was bound and posted off for marking. At this stage I was only interested in the finish of my journey and what it had meant to me and not the final grade. That said, I was driving my car when I received a call from the University confirming that I had passed. All of a sudden, in that moment, I had regressed; it was all about the result. I was now a "reformed academic", another behavioural change. These behavioural changes that I was experiencing were linked to my changing values.

Coaching Courses

The management team at the leadership school, including the external consultant, all met to discuss how could we ensure that the training transfer takes place within each respective organization? How could we now get the students from the TTT to continue their performance achieved on the TTT when they are back at their respective companies?

We discussed a number of options and finally agreed on setting up a series of coaching programs that could be placed alongside their respective company management framework. This would then involve developing a coaching system that could be used in each organization but adopted with specific individual's needs, but with the leadership school still remaining within a consultancy role.

We thought at the time: we had these students from the TTT who were going to coach learners on their performance and be responsible for their performance. But who was going to be responsible for the students' performance, we knew that there would be a management system in place, but what is in place from a leadership perspective, have they had any coach training at this level?

This was interesting as the school had conducted research and found that there were lots of organizations who were saying they were actively involved in coaching, but really they were focused either at the lowest level or the highest level and nothing had been placed over the entire organization.

There was nothing set up for the middle management, nothing for those individuals who are responsible for coaching the coach. Using this as guide we set out to develop a coach the coach programme to address this issue. In essence we developed a programme coaching a level up, a coaching framework.

The coach the coach framework sounded simple; just design a programme to meet the analysis gap, and this would be job done. Of course this was a lot easier said than done. At the time the leadership school was looking at creating something that hadn't really been done before.

We needed expert advice that agreed with the external consultant. It was decided that we approach Sir John Whitmore[5] as he was seen as the industry lead in this field of coaching. He agreed to provide that top level strategic consultancy that was required and the coach the coach programme was born.

The coach the coach programme that was designed was a framework of coaching that could be placed over the organization. It worked from the lowest end of the management chain, all the way to the top of the management chain including the CEO of respective organizations.

This framework still had in place the leadership school, which, would act as the starting point for the framework. The leadership school would serve as the consultancy piece throughout the framework design, and implementation in each respective company. The framework could be adapted to meet the individual company management frameworks as required.

I would go on to adapt this framework for the consultancy that I would be responsible for, after leaving the leadership school. In the coaching framework diagram I am

---

[5] Regarded by many as being responsible for modern day coaching.

represented as "author".

The Coaching Framework:

Coaching Hierarchy

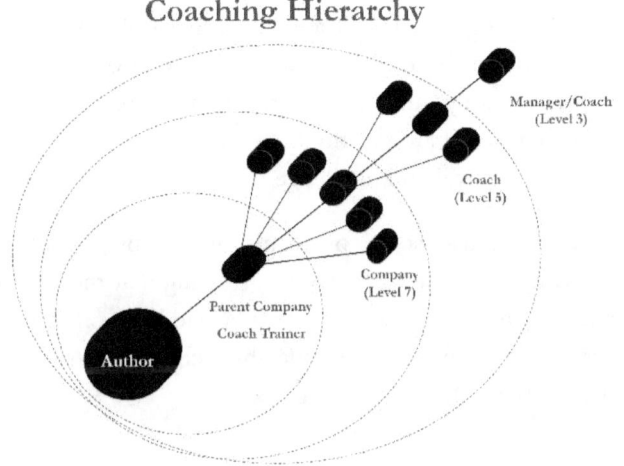

Having created the coach the coach programme it provided the leadership school with the next big question: if you had coaches that were coaching the coach, who was coaching the coach that was coaching the coach? This was a bigger dilemma as now you were working with individuals who were responsible for the strategic direction that companies were to operate at?

If you look at the Institute for Leadership and Management (ILM) as an example they have accredited programs that are at the right levels and that are delivered by a number of high level organizations and universities as an example. But on closer examination of the objectives and outcomes of a number of their internal products and programs they fall into that life coaching bracket and not performance related for the company.

By looking at accreditation you are having at some point having to modifying the programme to meet the accreditation, so it becomes about the accreditation and not the program. The leadership school also found that you end up becoming reliant on the SME from the awarding body understanding the new material that is designed, so where did the SME from the awarding body get there equivalent knowledge from?

This did cause some problems at the time, with one individual from an awarding body saying that they had not covered this on the course that they had been on. This was exactly the point that the leadership school was suggesting, they were creating something new.

This coach the coach programme had to be designed from scratch to meet this strategic overview at the right level so that individuals within each organization could provide the correct level of coaching advice, direction and overview. The 'Master' coach was had now been created to act as the strategic and organizational change at the highest strategic level.

Both the Coach the Coach and Master Coach programs had a large resource commitment within the workplace, which meant that I had to become the leadership and coaching expert in all fields at the leadership school. There would be no room for cutting and pasting. This time I had to do it for real. It was time for me to develop myself, and step-up and become the leadership SME.

Chapter 3 – Leadership

What is Leadership?

What is leadership? What does the word leadership mean? We often say we use it; some even think they are experts at using it. I was at the leadership school, responsible for the leadership delivery, implementation and instruction, but I had yet to define it. I had noticed while undertaking my academic journey the sheer vastness of leadership literature out there. Which leadership model is the right one to adopt? If you were to search for "leadership books" in Amazon, you get over twenty-two thousand hits.

Most people can talk about leadership, but few really understand it; most people want to achieve it. When you start to examine it, it always surprises me how quickly one word can illicit such an emotional response in people. Right now as you are reading this, you will be having an internal emotional debate, already talking to yourself, explaining that you already know what leadership is. You are drawing from your past experiences and formulating your own internal model of it.

The first thing that I will do is define what leadership is in order to position and explain the secret. Here is a group activity that you can try – use a flip chart and ask the group to come with a definition of leadership. Get the group to write down their individual group definitions. Then have a look at the definitions that the group give. You will rarely get any two groups with the same definition.

This is the difficulty in trying to define leadership. This was a puzzle for me at the time in the leadership school too. How could you define something that has so many different meanings to so many people and organizations, especially if they have been exposed to different styles of leadership in the past.

The next time you walk into a book shop, go to the business section and look up books on leadership, there will be several leadership books that all explain what leadership is. How do you define the leadership that will work for you? This at the time was the burning question that I had. How would I be able to consult on leadership if I was yet to define it for myself? Which model of leadership would be the best one for me to adopt?

I was fortunate, as at this time the leadership school had started to work on the model of leadership that the school would adopt. There had been previous academic research that had taken place in aligning leadership and the values of the organization (Hardy and Arthur, 2006) leading to examination of the results in relation to performance. This was key, as I would be looking to increase performance.

Values Based Leadership

The leadership school would go on to define leadership as Values Based Leadership (VBL). This term VBL would form the model of leadership I would go on to adopt. Before I can explain what VBL is I needed to find out what was a value, and why were they important within leadership?

Understanding what a value is was important in understanding the model VBL. It is important to understand a little of the leadership thinking that has got me to the VBL model and the learning that got me there on my leadership journey. This will place in the foundations to understanding the leadership secret.

Values

What do you think of when someone asks you to name an example of a value? I have often asked myself the same question and I'm sure that like me you think the traditional values that are commonly mentioned such as loyalty, discipline, integrity and love as examples.

It turns out that values are the specific belief systems that we have about that which is most important to us. Here is the first dilemma in setting values: you have to be honest with yourself, and if you're not honest with yourself then you cannot place value on your own values. Asking yourself to be honest is difficult, as you may not like your own answer.

They are the fundamental, ethical, moral and practical judgments that we make about what is right and wrong. This is our internal moral compass and it guides us accordingly. As such, values direct our motivation and, in the same way, can be described as either toward or away from. Similarly, whether operating at the conscious level or unconscious level, they guide our every decision and ultimately determine our behaviour and results.

This was a very important discovery, that values could have an impact on results, and our behaviour towards them. My behaviour had changed attending the previous courses whilst at the leadership school; this must have meant that my values had to have changed in order to get the change in behaviour.

What happens, however, if you do not have a clear idea as to what is most important to yourself and what your values are? As a result of this you may do things and, then afterwards, you find that you are unhappy with yourself. This is a type of "internal conflict" that arises because of opposing sets of values that conflict with each other. Although you might take action at one level (conscious), there is a part of you (unconscious) that does not believe that what you are doing is right.

This type of internal conflict invariably results in failure and you end up feeling bad about yourself. How many times have you not really tried at something and then, when you don't get the result, you feel bad about yourself?

Not about the result but knowing you could have done better yourself. This is often the case at work, at school and or perhaps going to the gym as an example.

In order to get the results that we want in our lives, we have to have a clear and fundamental sense of who we are, what really matters. This is all pretty straight forward, but how do we get our employees to take on the values if the organization doesn't believe in them themselves? This is going to have a direct impact on the performance of the company.

This reminds me of a time I was asked to look at the results of a large organization within the United Arab Emirates (UAE) for a large government company. They had invested considerable money in the creation of their values and the behaviours that they wanted but weren't getting the behaviour from their majority of the staff. When I looked into this, I discovered that the values and the behaviours that they had designed were functional and relevant to the company and designed well.

The issue I discovered was that although the senior management had all the relevant training, and understood the values and behaviours, similar training had not been delivered to the majority of the work force. It had been disseminated by internal email or marketing that most employees hadn't seen or taken any notice of.

My advice to them was that they didn't need me at all that, in order to see the behaviour desired they had to first disseminate the values by training to all members of staff, in the similar fashion that they had given to the senior management. This was common sense, but was now asking some difficult questions of the organization – such as did they truly value their own workforce? If they did they wouldn't have needed me to show them.

The key then is getting individuals to connect to the values, especially if companies values are different to that of the individual. What is needed is that emotional connection to the value. I often see this in values, that although they have been designed well, the relevance and dissemination within the company has not been thought about in the same detail. I have also seen too often companies getting the behaviour mixed up with the values. This has an effect when the value is the behaviour, not a value.

Beliefs

Linking values to our behaviours are our beliefs, what are our beliefs? Research suggests beliefs are the knowledge structures, located in the brain memory, that contain our experience of ourselves, other people, and the world in which we live. As such, they give us a sense of certainty in an uncertain world, allowing us to anticipate what will happen in given situations, and guide and facilitate our behaviour.

Values, meanwhile, are the specific belief systems we have about what is most important to us, and incorporate the fundamental, ethical, moral and practical judgments we make about what is right and wrong. Fundamentally, these things not only determine who we are, but what we are capable of. We therefore have a vested interest in understanding them so that we can control them rather than have them control us.

Armed with this definition of values and beliefs, it was important that I understand what effect beliefs could have on performance, and all of the books that I had been reading at that time suggested that these beliefs are split into limiting and empowering beliefs.

Empowering and Limiting Beliefs

It occurred to me, that our beliefs play an important role in determining our performance, so I looked at some successful individuals and what made them successful. I couldn't imagine Richard Branson sat there at the beginning and thinking that he was going to fail, when he created the Virgin brand.

Imagine a football manager addressing their team prior to a big game, coming off the back of a previous loss. Although they have just had a negative result, they don't plan on getting another failure, the address to the team is still about winning the next game, it's about planning for success and not failure.

People who succeed in life differ greatly in their beliefs from those that fail. Our beliefs about who we are, and who we can be, determine what we will be. If we believe in a life of opportunity, we invariably live a life of opportunity. If we believe our life is defined by narrow limits, then we invariably make those limits real.

What we believe to be true or possible becomes what is true or possible. It is an example of the self fulfilling cycle; if I believe I won't or can't then I don't get the results. If I believe I can I am more likely to succeed, even if I don't get the initial results I'm looking for, I accept that I will get them.

I would go on to understand the difference between limiting and empowering beliefs. Beliefs can either be empowering or limiting. Whilst an empowering belief is one that facilitates our happiness, growth, and fulfilment, a limiting belief inevitably stops us from realizing our true potential.

We can usually identify which of our beliefs are empowering and limiting by reflecting upon the language that we use to describe them. Typically we describe our empowering beliefs in terms of "I'm good at", "I like" or "I can". Similarly, we usually describe our limiting beliefs in terms of "I'm no good at", "I don't like" and "I can't."

If I could understand these powerful beliefs were linked to my values I could use this information to impact on performance? If I knew that I had a limiting belief, what could I do to change it into a empowering belief? Similarly, if a organization is made up of a culture of it "can't be done", "it will never change", "we always do it that way". Then what could be done to change the belief system to that of a empowering one?

Later I would be in involved with a high performance organization that worked on a ten percent pass rate as its performance bench mark. They had approached me to increase the pass rate. I had started to dig into the organization and the beliefs and values that were evident.

I found that they believed that that they had always got a

ten percent pass rate and that no matter what they did, they would always get a ten percent pass rate. They also believed that if the pass rate went up that they would be seen as the ones who had dropped the standard in order to increase the pass rate.

By addressing the beliefs and turning their limiting beliefs into empowering ones, demonstrating that there would be no drop in standard and that the results were performance driven, the organization was able to deliver an increase to a sixteen percent first time pass rate.

This sounded great, but caused a whole new set of issues, as the rest of the organization had only been preparing for the ten percent that they normally had passing, now there was an additional six percent, a nice problem to have though.

Leadership Thinking

Armed with this new found knowledge on values I turned my attention to leadership, investigating leadership theory that had evolved over the years. In order to build up this knowledge I needed to understand how we had got to where we are today in current leadership thinking. I had to explore the theory of leadership thinking and discover where we are today in relation to this thinking.

I needed to research leadership history. This was daunting at first, as I had mentioned earlier, the amount of leadership literature that was out there. I started to ask other people that I respected about where did they go for references in their leadership development.

At times I got back the standard reply of 'erm uhm you know it's that thing, it's where we do this, where we do that.' Getting an answer on where I could go to research leadership history was equally as hard as asking what does the word leadership mean mentioned earlier.

I had to really search and seek out credible individuals that were impartial and not selling their own history or view of the history of leadership. Through this research I had managed to find the following snap shot of the history of leadership thinking, whilst remaining as impartial as possible without any bias:

Great Man – based on a belief that leaders are exceptional people born with innate qualities, destined to lead. If you study their lives you can emulate them. Problem is that great leaders such as Ghandi, Thatcher, Churchill and Mandela display widely different personal qualities. Studying a person is one thing, being able to copy them is another.

The Trait - approach abandons linking leadership qualities with particular individuals and lists a number of traits or characteristics which are believed to relate to effective leadership. However, studies have failed to find any link between effective leadership and any single characteristic.

Behaviourist - theories focus on what leaders really do and the differences between effective and non-effective leaders. This is an avenue where you can look at styles of leadership.

Situational - leadership is about the specific context in which leadership is being exercised. For example, military leadership may demand skills, qualities and behaviours which differ from those associated with leadership in industry.

Transactional - emphasizes the importance of the relationship between leaders and followers, focusing on the mutual benefits derived from a form of "contract" through which the leader delivers rewards or recognition in return for the commitment or loyalty of the followers. This is the most widely used leadership style and it seems the easiest one to adopt.

Transformational - theory, the central concept is still about a relationship between leader and led, but is about creating a vision, having shared values and obtaining commitment to change. Mutual trust is the key to being a transformational leader.

This was my brief glimpse into my research in leadership thinking. Modern examples of individuals that are linked to leadership success, are Gates, Jobbs and Branson to name but a few. There has been a shift to move away from the military leaders of the past, that were associated with leadership thinking.

Leadership Styles

It seemed that after taking a fast track look at leadership thinking I had ended up at transactional and transformation leadership; these were first identified by James McGregor Burns in 1978. They were spectrums of opposites on a scale on which you could place, leadership. Transactional leadership produces change at the psychological level of actions and results, to change what people "do".

Transformational leadership produces change at the psychological level of values and beliefs to change how people "think". This level of change suggests that the person, not just their behaviour, has been changed or "transformed".

In order to get an idea for the spectrum of leadership styles through transactional and transformational leadership I found that six leadership styles (Daniel Goleman, 1990) were researched in having impact on the climate of an organization and of those being led.

Currently, transformational leadership is the buzz word within leadership, but was identified over three decades ago, and it is only now that individuals and organizations are looking to implement a wide spectrum of different styles in leadership. It highlights that if it has taken this long for them to wake up to the possibility of change within leadership how sometimes barriers that are evident during organizational change can take a long time to break down.

It is important at this stage to let you know that these styles of leadership that Goleman looked at are not the definitive styles of leadership, just examples of styles of leadership that fitted the best for the VBL model that was created. Language is important as they are examples 'of' and not 'the' examples. From a consultancy perspective, if there were others that fitted or seemed to fit a given situation, then these could have been adopted.

In order to develop the VBL, it was important to look at the styles in more detail, since these styles form an important element in the VBL model, and similarly I had to explore them in the same way that I had approached the leadership thinking, whilst remaining impartial. It was important that I looked at them as individuals styles initially, and Goleman suggested the following styles, which I have expanded to fit in with the VBL model:

Directive Leadership: "Tell: Do what I tell you"

This leadership style demands immediate compliance from the work force or individuals. Certainly there is a feel of 'Just do it' – I'm the boss, there is little room for negotiation. Tight control is exercised by the leader. It involves a lot negative feedback – 'you didn't do that right'; which can often lead to a fear of failure syndrome.

This is not particularly useful if trying to implement a culture of change. It can result in new ideas being stifled; cooperation falls, and inflexibility is often evident.

That said, this style of leadership is a very good approach in a crisis situation with a competent team. You may have seen this style used by Sir Alan Sugar on the television show the Apprentice[6] – where he explains exactly what he wants to see.

Visionary or Authoritative Leadership: "Sell: Come with me"

---

[6] *The Apprentice* is a British reality game show in which a group of aspiring businessmen and women compete for the chance to work with the British business magnate Alan Sugar

This style of leadership mobilizes people towards a vision, it is firm but fair: "come with me" outlook. It is based on a development of a clear agreed vision, clear standards and feedback. It explains the rationale for procedures that need to be adopted within the organization or by the individual. It can be motivating; as it explains the 'why' but leaves the 'how' to team members.

This is very empowering for the team members. Praise outweighs criticism, with clear meaningful goals established from the beginning with long term direction. Team members see how their task fits into the bigger picture. This style of leadership is a favourite with film makers, as when linked to music it can produce powerful emotions. Who can forget the opening words to a very successful film and television franchise - "Space, the final frontier…"[7]

Pacesetting leadership: "Do as I do, now!" - or I'll do it myself."

In this particular style the team leader sets high standards for performance, and leads by example. Subordinates are unlikely to innovate incase the standards fall and the task s taken from them. As a result of this there is often reluctant delegation with an obsession about doing things better, faster and quicker. It does, however, pinpoint poor performance and then as a result it can eradicate it.

A pacesetters demand for excellence can sometimes overwhelm a number of team members as sometimes there is a thought that although they can do that, there is

---

[7] Star Trek

no way that I will be able to do it. Poor performance is normally not tolerated, with any form of praise rarely used.

There is not normally any vision created, and it looks towards the short term only. Because of this there is a tendency to be a lack of coordination, which often means that the big picture is lost.

One of the ways that I picture this style of leadership is on some sort of instruction as if you are part of a well oiled machine, perhaps learning to be a fireman for example, where you are taught a little, practice a little, and so on. Evident during instructor lead teaching for a new skill.

Affliliative Leadership: "People first, task second"

This style of leadership creates harmony and strong emotional bonds. Often though there is a lack of challenge that is then compromised by the desire to keep other team members happy. Harmony within the team ends up more important than standards. This can have a direct impact on performance.

With the affiliative style there is usually undifferentiated praise given, and this is normally for fear of upsetting another team member. Little explanation on direction or rationale behind tasks is given as focus on praise can allow poor performance to go unchecked. In organizations that adopt this style, standards may be low so all can achieve the required performance. A lack of clear advice or direction can leave team members floundering.

I often reflect thinking that this type of leadership, when used, reminds me more of a conversation. Think about how you would build relationships and rapport with people. How did your weekend go? Is your wife feeling better? And so on.

Participative Leadership: "What do you think?"

This style of leadership uses the 'what do you think?' approach where by ideas are encouraged on a grand scale; collaboration and team agreement is often sought out. There is a need for consensus, which may compromise effort and success within the team. Because there is a high reliance on trust, respect and commitment this can lead to decisions being delayed for too long until central agreements can be reached.

Because everyone is involved they all share the rewards, and this then discourages differential discretionary effort. There is a tendency for this style to lead to confusion and lack of direction in time of crisis

Certain government styles of council will often practice this style of leadership. As will meetings at boardroom level within industry.

Coaching leadership: "What if you could?" Or "Try this" or "Ask, don't tell"

This style of leadership is covered in the next chapter, but in essence it encourages dialogue within the organization and looks to the future. It involves developing others, and does not assume one 'font of all knowledge' for everyone. The leaders will help other team members to discover their own strengths and weaknesses, and as a result will develop specific needs.

This will sometimes lead to standards dropping in the short term whilst team members 'try things out' and develop the required new skills.

There has to be regular feedback and positive reinforcement throughout and the delivery of the feedback is key – there is a real sense that team leaders care about the future of their workforce. The long term development and future-proofing is important, which leads to it being adapted to fit other parts of the organization.

Initially it may be a time consuming style and it needs a degree of expertise from the leader, which has to be taught or developed. There may be some instances of team members being very resistant to learning or changing or developing as they may see this as a threat.

Individuals find it strange that one of the people who emphasizes the hard edges of the coaching style is Gordon Ramsay[8]. Many people would associate him with the more coercive elements, but if you look at what he does when he is in a kitchen, there is a huge amount of really honest feedback. He thinks about people's vision for their restaurant and helps them to reach their goals; it is not about him saying what he would do.

Another thing about coaching as a leadership style is the fact that we use it as a leadership style. Often people refer to leadership and coaching or management and coaching, but I had realized earlier that it is not the case, it is just a

---

[8] Gordon Ramsay is known for presenting TV programs about competitive cookery and food, such as the British series *Hell's Kitchen*, *The F Word*, and *Ramsay's Kitchen Nightmares*

part of leadership. A training company won't tell you this as this is one of the ways that they make more money out of selling you training programs that you don't really need based in leadership and management.

The Golf Bag

In order to contextualize these leaderships styles together for this example, I'm going to use the six styles that was suggested earlier, that have been briefly explained. We have to determine which one is the best? The title of the book is based on a leadership secret, so here is a little secret on the styles of leadership that you won't find in any of the books or with the consultants you may have come across.

Certainly, at the moment coaching is a strong 'buzz' word, so if you are talking to a coach they of course are going to suggest that coaching would be the most appropriate one to use. In fact, the secret of any leadership style is that they all work, they all get results! But which one to use, and when to use it?

Imagine now, that you are a top golfer, and you're playing in the United States PGA Open. You are standing on the first tee and the green is some five hundred and seventy five yards away. Don't worry if you have never played before, just picture that you need to take the biggest club out of the golf bag and hit the ball as hard as you can, and as straight as you can.

You address the ball[9] and hit it as hard as you can,

---

[9] Golfing terminology.

unfortunately, although you hit it over three hundred yards, it falls to the right in the long grass.

As you walk up to the ball, having spent ten minutes searching for it, you now have to get the golf ball back on to the fairway. So you need select a smaller club from the golf bag. You hit the ball out of the long grass, but although you are progressing towards the green you land in a bunker, which is full of sand.

Now you need to look into the golf bag, and take out the club that has been specially designed to get the ball out of the sand. Again you address the ball and you manage to hit it out of the sand and it lands on the green. Inside the golf bag is a club called a putter that has been designed so you can tap the ball into the hole. After three taps you manage to get the ball into the hole.

What has this got to do with our leadership styles? The way I approach this, is that we carry around with us a leadership "golf bag", and I need to stress again that no single style is thought to be the best, but like a good golfer the good leader varies appropriate style according to situation and team member concerned. Just the same way that you would select the club as mentioned earlier, to get the golf ball into the hole.

Thinking about this Golf Club analogy – what is your most effective leadership club? In other words, what is the most effective 'club' you have in your leadership golf bag? Which one do you understand the most? Which one do you least understand?

The thing to remember is: whether playing golf or leading

– we need to get results, by selecting the most appropriate golf club (leadership style), that we need to get the ball into the hole. It just happens that the coaching style is the one that is least understood, with the direct style being the traditionally easier one to adopt.

Values Based Leadership

If I now go back to VBL, and how it was created, what does it look like? How can we use VBL? In order to demonstrate VBL you need to think about the behaviours that you want from an organization. For this example I am going to construct the metaphor of a building, and build the VBL model around it.

Once we have these behaviours, they can be placed at the top of the building. The values are placed at the bottom. Imagine a house with the roof acting as the behaviours and the values as the foundations. Supporting walls need to be created to ensure that the building will stand up, these are our leadership styles.

In essence we have our behaviours, which are taken from the leadership style that is adopted, which is underpinned by the values, hence the term Values Based Leadership. The point is, that if we were to look down on top of the building, the part that we see is the behaviour.

VBL is based on strong foundations that enable the wanted behaviours to be applied, using the appropriate leadership style to fit each unique situation. As these styles are used as a "skill" they can be each developed, and performance improved in each.

Representation of Values Based Leadership:

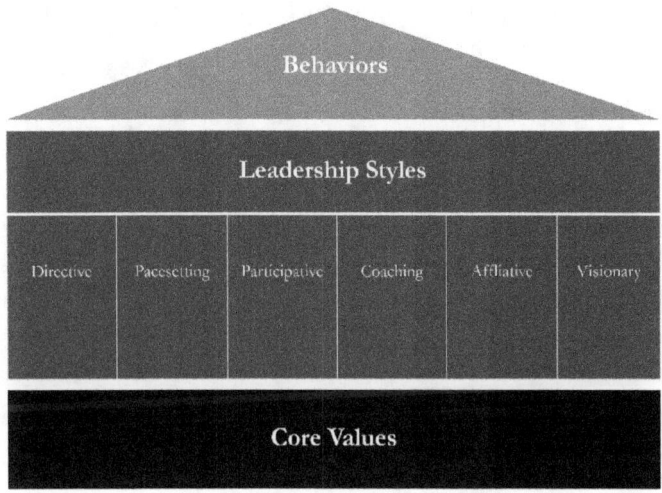

If we are feeling stressed we would normally revert to the style of leadership that we feel most comfortable with. Ask yourself which style of leadership do you feel most comfortable using from the examples given earlier? Which style do you think you see most when people or organizations are stressed?

Nine times out of ten it's going to be more of a transactional style from the spectrum of those styles. They are the most easily adopted. Here then is the thing though: they all get results, it doesn't matter which style that is adopted, they all get results. Some may get you results quicker, some may get you there with more empowerment, some may get you there with an angry workforce.

It doesn't matter, they will all eventually bring you the result; it's how you get there that is really important. The more transformational styles such as coaching are great for results but are the least understood.

Having completed research into different styles of leadership, I was now satisfied with the concept of leadership related to the model of VBL, and the leadership thinking that got me there, I was also armed with my leadership golf bag.

I know that by asking these questions of myself within the VBL model, I was comfortable with the transactional styles, but now realized that I was not so comfortable with the coaching styles. I needed to fully understand them and develop them so that I felt equally comfortable. I needed to get on the leadership driving range and reduce my leadership handicap.[10]

The Leadership Secret

Being the title of the book it is only fitting that I cover the leadership secret within the leadership chapter. This seems the fitting place to cover it. I have now shown you how leadership thinking ended up with the VBL model. The thing is not to say that VBL is the definitive leadership theory, of course not, it is a blend of leadership theories that fit where we are today in current leadership thinking linked to values and behaviours.

---

[10] Golfing analogy to reduce your score and increase performance.

If I think back to when my grandparents were young I think that they had a stronger values set than that of the majority of young people now. Society has changed, technology is changing every day, perhaps there wasn't a need for VBL in the past. But today, in a world that is ever shrinking, how do we ensure common values and shared goals in our organizations?

VBL plays a part in aligning this and ensuring performance in the workplace. Imagine a large multinational company that recruits from all over the world: all the employees bring with them a value set from their respective countries and cultures, however, when they work at the company they are expected to behave in a way that supports the values of the company. When we place this together we have the leadership secret, the ugly truth - which I will cover later.

In order to reveal the leadership secret, it is important that I contextualize it in the remaining chapters so that it can be fully understood. If not then this would be a very small book. I can see it in you now that you want to turn to the end to discover the secret. I know that this is what you want to do. On some level we all want to know what it is.

Here is a quick experiment that you can try:place a box of chocolates on a coffee table and bring in some children aged say 3 – 6 as an example and explain to them that whatever they do they are not to eat any of the chocolate from the box, and then leave them to play. If you then 'spy' on them and watch the interaction then at some point one or all will eventually eat a chocolate. They cannot resist, they have to.

M A. Grant

Chapter 4 – Coaching

What is Coaching

Within this research into leadership, I had discovered that 'coaching' would often appear, and not from a sporting context, which it is most commonly associated with. I had discovered as previously mentioned, on the course conducted by the external consultant, that it was a leadership style, before I had undertaken the research I would have previously thought that it was "leadership and coaching."

Coaching is now the must-have skill for the modern leader or manager, and if you have ever applied for a job recently you will notice that it has appeared on most job descriptions, finding its way in to Key Performance

Indicators (KPIs). I certainly needed this particular skill in my golf bag if I was to become a effective leadership SME. But what was coaching?

There seemed to be lots of books written on coaching, and depending on which book you read would determine the coaching style that would be adopted. There are thousands of training companies that are willing to take your money, all professing to be 'gurus' in coaching, and that in one or two days they could get you at the top of the coaching game.

For me this is concerning, since if they were this good at coaching, then there would be no need to take my hard earned cash for two days they would be delivering this in business themselves as this is where the perception of money is.

If you looked for individuals that coach for performance within businesses and organizations, the list of coaches shortens, as most coaches work around the model of life coaching. Life coaching is a different style of coaching compared to coaching for performance within industry.

If you were the CEO of a large organization looking to implement coaching would you want an individual with no commercial experience that was very young coaching your company? The coaches have to start somewhere, but after a two day course the training companies that train these coaches, convince them that they are now equipped to take on this role. Most coaches that coach in performance usually make the step into coaching having previously held positions of authority in industry.

When I started to research coaching I discovered that a number of individuals and books would reference Sir Jon Whitmore and the GROW tool, which is covered later in this chapter, as the basic or primary coaching tool. It would be wrong not to recommend this tool too, my advice would be buy the book: Coaching for Performance by Sir John Whitmore.

This book I would highly recommend serving as a technical book on coaching for those who wish specialize in coaching. As I mentioned earlier I was lucky enough to have met Sir John on a number of occasions. He was an invited member of the executive committee for the leadership school. In this chapter I will explain what coaching is, and in real terms how to use it for performance, linked to the model of VBL.

Like all styles of leadership, and skills that you may use or new concepts, you have to come up with a definition, you have to define what it is that you are doing, for what purpose? Therefore it was important to determine the definition of coaching that would be adopted as part of VBL.

The UK Government use the following definition to explain coaching: Coaching is the key to unlocking potential in order to maximize performance. This had been designed to fit around the coaching programs of the leadership school. You could 'Google' coaching definitions until you seem to find the one that fits for you if required.

I like this one as it has the key elements that had been designed to fit in the VBL model, which is potential and performance. Coaching is about taking potential and turning it into performance. Certainly within industry, organizations are looking for performance, which they can look to get return on any investment made.

I had been coaching this for a long time but hadn't realized this is was what I had been doing, I hadn't realized that I had been 'coaching', it was something that I had just done. If you think about this I have just given the definition, but what did we do before called it coaching? How did we get performance out of individuals or organizations without coaching?

Of course we did coach this, we just didn't call it coaching, we may have called it common sense or something similar, but it is important to note that coaching isn't something new. Individuals and organizations have been doing it for a long time, achieving some credible results. Later I will cover "goals", but what did we do before the word "goal" was used?

We still set goals, just under a different name. Perhaps the process had always been there, the language over time has changed. Anyone who has children will appreciate that they speak a completely different language now compared to when we were young, (lol, gr8, m8[11]).

Goals

What is a goal? How many times have you heard this word used in the modern workplace, or even in the home? "What is a goal?" is fundamental as it turns out that goal

---

[11] Laugh out Loud, Great and Mate.

setting is the key to successful performance, and it's the primary tool for getting results.

A goal can be described as whatever a person is trying to accomplish, the aim, object or target of their actions. This means that our goals typically relate to the achievement of a specific outcome or result, that which a person "wants", and usually involves a specific timeframe.

Goal setting, meanwhile, refers to the process of setting goals. It suggests that there is a specific method for getting the results we want. This is true if we look at following our dreams and having aspirations as forms of goal setting, but these processes are much more intuitive than proper goal setting.

By turning our dreams and aspirations into goals, and following the goal setting process, we are much better placed to turn our goals into reality. We could spend the first half of our lives thinking this is what I want to achieve, and the second half thinking I wish I had achieved this.

I discovered that there are generally three types of goals that are important in the process of goal setting, and these can be used independently or they can be used in conjunction with one another, these are:

Outcome goals: These goals usually relate to the dreams and aspirations from which the goal originated and are often expressed as a mission statement or vision. They are usually described subjectively in terms of emotion and are concerned with why the goal is important. Outcome goals are important for motivation and commitment.

Performance goals: These goals relate to a predetermined standard against which achievement can be measured. They are described objectively in terms of cognition and are concerned with what the goal actually is. Performance goals are very important for focus, control and recognition of goal attainment.

Process goals: These goals relate to what needs to be done in order to make the goal a reality. They are described prescriptively in terms of behaviour and are concerned with how the goal actually is to be achieved. Large process goals are normally broken down into interim or sub goals. Process goals are important for monitoring what works and what doesn't work.

SMART Principles

Smarter principles, or SMART, is a useful tool that aids in ensuring that the goal is achieved. You will have noticed that SMART is now used in the workplace, and it is commonly used outside of coaching terms, which is testament to the fact that SMART works, but what does it stand for and how do we make it smarter?

I would have liked to take the credit for this but this is all down to Sir John Whitmore, and it is still as relevant today as it was when he first published it.

The acronym SMART is a useful tool with which to remember the fundamental principles of effective goal setting, exploring our goals more fully, and ensuring that they are clearly and precisely defined as possible. They are as follows:

Specific: Goals should be always be clearly and positively defined in terms that are behavioural. In this way, they should relate to outcomes and actions that are specific rather than ones that are general. Rather than simply saying that we are going to be a better manager or that we are going to get fitter, we should be looking to describe in exactly what way we are going to be a better manager and in exactly what way we are going to get fitter.

An example I get with young graduates is that they want to be the CEO. I then have to dig down to make it as specific as possible, the CEO of what organization? Which company do you want to be the CEO of? Otherwise it ends up being just a general comment, 'I want to be a CEO.'

Measurable: Goals should be measurable, such that they set a benchmark, that can be used to monitor progress. In order to do so, we should be asking ourselves how we will know when we are a better manager? How will we know when we are fitter?

If we look at the goal setting process as a path that we intend to follow, we need to know where the path starts and where the path ends. We also need to have established milestones along the way, in order to ensure that we are not deviating from the path that we have chosen.

Look at the CEO comment, how could this be measured? If I am dealing with graduates, and the goal is to be the CEO of a specific company, one way that could demonstrate the measure: is in the form of promotions. Each promotion would stack up and demonstrate that the goal is measurable. In the workplace, the achievement of

KPIs could also serve as a measure of performance.

Achievable: Many people or organizations set goals that are completely out of reach for them or knowingly impossible to achieve. Although this practice is clearly self-defeating, many people do this in order to have a built-in excuse for not achieving their goals.

We must always have a realistic chance of reaching our goals, combined with a belief that we can reach them, in order to stay committed to them. This is the essence of "realistic" goal setting, although we must be careful how we use this term, extraordinary things are not achieved by realistic people!

Take the graduate again. It would be perfectly feasible that if they are young and just starting in the company that the position of CEO is attainable, however, if an individual's is in their mid fifties and they are starting at the bottom of the company and it takes on average 35 years to become the CEO, then this specific goal may not be attainable. The use of goal setting is a powerful tool in the management of expectations.

Repeatable: Fundamentally, performance and achievement are a process of "constant and never-ending improvement." As such, our goals should reflect this by being long-term. Short-term and intermediate goals (sub-goals), meanwhile, provide useful "stepping stones" that can help us to maintain our focus.

In order to do this, however, our goals not only have to be measurable – they need to be repeatable too. This also helps in monitoring our progress towards our goals. The graduate looking at promotion in the forms of measure, what steps did they take to achieve the first promotion?

If they then repeat these actions then the second promotion should follow, as I have demonstrated a proven action and performance. Could you also use this in another part of the workplace to repeat performance? When results come in and are repeatable they can spread very quickly and an organization can add substantial increases to the bottom line through repeatable performance.

Timed: In order for our goals to be measured in any real way they need to be timed. All too often individuals and organizations have goals that they are going to commit to "someday". Goals such as these are very rarely achieved, and certainly not within the timeframe originally intended.

Having developed an action plan they should immediately place a "start" and "achievement" date on the goals and use this time scale to monitor progress. This is important in long term career planning and management of expectations. It also means individuals can alter the goal or plan accordingly especially if they are seeing results quicker than anticipated.

The Coaching Process

Within coaching it's important to make sure that a process is followed. This process that would be adopted, needed to support coaching tools such as the GROW tool, it should fit over most things that we do in the workplace, but adapted for coaching.

The process that was created starts at the bottom and the

works upwards like climbing a ladder, and in order to get to the top you need to complete each step, and if you try to skip a step you could slip, or if not taken properly you could slip therefore it is important to take the logical steps, the process is as follows:

Raise Awareness: The beginning step of the coaching process is raising awareness. During this initial step you have to help the person or organization to create a vision of their goal (objective) in terms of what they want to achieve, what would be a reason to why they might want to achieve it? How do they intend to do so?

It is important that throughout this first step that the emphasis is on guiding the person or individual towards finding their own solutions to their own performance problems. Particularly for an individuals or organization, as it works for both. In this way, raising awareness is about getting the person to think for themselves for the act of raising the awareness. If you end up having to tell rather than ask then the goal is normally your goal and not theirs, and for this reason they have to come up with it for themselves.

Generate Responsibility: The next step of the coaching process is to get the person or organization to generate responsibility. During this step it is important to challenge the person or organization to take action towards making their goal a reality. In this way, generating responsibility is about getting the person or organization to feel they want to achieve it for themselves.

If they are unwilling to do this then they are not going to really want to do it. If there is a problem in generating responsibility, then you may have to go back to raising awareness. You cannot progress to the next step in the process without generating responsibility.

Facilitate Performance: The next step in the process is to facilitate the performance of the individual or organization. This usually takes place inside the workplace. During this step the idea is to support the person or organization as they take action towards making their goal a reality and deals with the challenge of doing so. In this way, facilitating performance is about getting the person to do for themselves.

This performance step is where all the magic happens, and I learned that in order to make the difference and allow training transfer it has to happen in the workplace. Have you ever been on a training course when the trainer then follow you back to the work place to ensure that you were then carrying out the actions taught from the course?

If you have to attend a course there should be at least an additional day for the follow up to ensure that this training transfer has taken place, it is also a great way to measure performance. In this way I learned that in order to get the performance

I had to go into the workplace and ensure training transfer was taking place, and from a coaching point of view, you cannot progress to the performance step until the first two have been climbed. If you do, you are probably not going to get the desired result or performance.

If you think about it logically, these three steps can be placed over most things in life or work. Imagine you want to bring in a new Human Resource (HR) system: the first thing you are going to do is raise awareness to the new system, and the part that everyone has to play in it. You would then have to generate responsibility for those people who are going to be using the system or involved in it.

Finally there will be the performance of using the new system. I can remember when I was younger, having had a new HR system that was to be implemented, and thinking that it will never work, but I was told that I was to use them anyway. After a period of time I realized that I had to use it, and then once I had accepted it became workable.

If I had got the first two steps in first I would have come to the same conclusion only earlier, which means the performance would have been achieved earlier. In business terms this would start to affect the bottom line. This was a real key realization for me, that I could use this process in business and within the act of consulting.

The Coaching Skills

Now that I understood and developed a process, there were a set of skills that are commonly used within coaching. These skills are the common skills used, and terminology may change, but in essence they are recognized within the coaching world, but not confined to. They are as follows:

Effective Questions: The primary coaching skill that is used in order to raise awareness during step one and two of the coaching process is the use of effective questioning.

In order to question effectively, in coaching the individual must employ a wide variety of questions and questioning techniques – including open and closed, broad and narrow, rhetorical and hypothetical, leading and interrogative, 50/50, and scale of 1-to-10 questions.

In order for these questions to be effective they must raise awareness and generate responsibility. It's at this stage that I began to practice my own effective question techniques. I practiced them everywhere, whether it was grabbing a coffee, doing the shopping or even speaking to my family. I notice that when I got it completely wrong there was that 'dazed' expression on an individual's face: the feedback is instant.

The more results and positive ones that I got, the more I developed a bank of questions that I could use and I could quickly formulate a question to the response that I got from individuals. For this reason, having the ability to ask effective questions is not only important in a coaching context, but can be used as effectively anywhere. Examples of coaching questions that I would use are:

What do you want to achieve?
What is important to you right now?
What would you like to get from the next 30 minutes?
What areas do you want to work on?
Describe your perfect world
What do you want to achieve as a result of this session?

Where are you now in relation to your goal?
On a scale of 1 -10 where are you?
What has contributed to your success so far?
What skills/knowledge/attributes do you have?

What progress have you made so far?
What is working well right now?

What are your options?
How have you tackled this/or had similar situation before?
What could you do differently?
Who do you know who has encountered a similar situation?
If anything was possible what would you do?
What else?

Which options work best for you?
What one small step are you going to take now?
What actions will you take?
When are you going to start?
Who will help you?
How will you know you have been successful?
How will you ensure that you do it?
On a scale of 1 -10 how committed /motivated are you to doing it?

Active Listening: The second skill employed in order to generate responsibility and raise awareness within the coaching process is active listening. In order to actively listen, an individual must first be silent, and then actively engage in the listening process as opposed to passively doing so. This is achieved by a process of "whole body" listening – employing the ears, the eyes, and the heart, in order to make sensory judgments about the person's levels of confidence and motivation.

This is certainly easier said than done. Have you ever been listening to someone's response to a question that you have asked, and you know the answer, yet they still haven't got it, your whole body just wants to scream out the answer! This skill, once you start to pick up on the small things, becomes easy to pick up the more you use, but it takes practice.

An example of this was I had to give an employee some good news that they were promoted, but the promotion would involve moving to a new part of the country. I explained to them that they were being promoted and that it would involve a move and asked the question "are you happy with that?" The response I got was "yes I am happy", but they were shaking their head at the same time, so they were telling me what I wanted to hear, but subconsciously they were telling me something different.

I questioned them on this and found out that they had children in a great school and had just bought a house, so although they wanted the promotion, the move away would be the worse decision at the present time for them given their personal circumstances.

Empathic Responding: When it comes to getting the performance, the skill used in order to facilitate performance during the process is empathic responding. Responding with empathy requires that an individual should have a true understanding of the person's needs before choosing the best response to them.

When responding with empathy it's important to give constructive feedback that builds, and it is always done constructively, even if the result is negative. This seems to go against the grain, and if you think about a time when you got a negative result and you got feedback, traditionally it is done using a transactional style, 'you didn't do this', 'you didn't do that', 'you should have done this', and so on, instead of building and using constructive feedback.

The use of validated praise is used, the validated the "reason why" , how many times have you completed a task and all you get is a well done or good job or words similar. By validating the reason, then you are showing that the reason was understood, for example: "that was a great result because I noticed this", and "you did this".

Otherwise it goes in one ear and out the other. How many times have you witnessed this at work, at home, at school or even with our own children, that when speaking at them they take no responsibility for their subsequent actions.

Emotional Quotient (EQ) & Intelligence Quotient (IQ)

We often refer to how intelligent we are by measuring our IQ, this is a familiar term for most of us. We can also apply this to our knowledge and skills and broadly place them as a representative of a person's IQ. However, linked to our knowledge and skills is our motivation, another way of looking at motivation is our attitude, which is broadly representative of a person's EQ.

Whereas IQ encompasses the verbal, logical-mathematical and visual-spatial intelligences typically taught formally at school through the process of education, EQ comprises the intra-personal and inter-personal intelligences typically learned informally through life experience and the process of socialization. This development of EQ has been led by the likes of Daniel Goleman and is now the subject of development programs in this field alone.

If you have a high EQ, then you're able to see your emotional state, as well as the emotional state of those around you, and draw them to you rather than push them away. You can use your understanding of their emotions in order to relate to them better, and form healthier relationships.

Goleman suggests, that our EQ is made up of the following: Self Awareness, Self Regulation, Motivation, Empathy and Social Skills. It's worth expanding on these, because once I understood what they meant I was able to better understand other people and how their respective EQ can be developed. This EQ could also be place into an organization and therefore has a role within the VBL Model:

Self Awareness: The ability to understand your strengths and own weaknesses, your internal motivations, drives and preferences, and how you appear to both yourself and other people. Basically understanding who you are.

Self Regulation: Based upon your own self-awareness, the ability to appropriately control the emotions that drive your behaviour in different situations, and if you think before you act. This is basically knowing right from wrong. It is ok to think it, but you know to act upon it is wrong.

Motivation: Based upon self-regulation, the ability to direct your internal resources, your knowledge, skills and attitudes, towards a predetermined outcome or goal. This can be internal and external depending on the situation or goal that needs to be achieved.

Empathy: Based upon motivation, the ability to understand the strengths and weakness of other people, their internal motivations, drives and preferences, and consider their needs and viewpoints. The way I look at this is walking in someone else's shoes but keeping your own socks on. Not to be confused with sympathy.

Social Skills: Based upon empathy, the ability to establish, maintain and develop relationships and communicate effectively to get what you want whilst respecting the rights of other people. This is the part that others see when looking at your EQ.

Why is EQ so Important?

EQ is very important for everyone. We know that individuals who are the smartest are not always the most successful, or the most fulfilled in their lives. We can probably recall someone who is academically brilliant, but they are not socially graceful, and unsuccessful in their work, or their personal relationships due to their ineptness.

Our intellectual intelligence is not enough for us to be successful and happy in life. Your IQ can get you into university, but your EQ is what will help you manage your emotions, and stress, when your facing exams.

Your EQ affects your work life significantly. If you have a high EQ, you can navigate the social complexities of your workplace, and lead or motivate others. You can excel in your chosen career. When it comes to gauging job candidates as an example, companies view EQ as more important than technical ability.

Developing my own EQ has helped me within all forms employment as a consultant and in general life, and therefore plays a part within coaching.[12]

The GROW Tool

Having established, the process and skills, it was important to have a deep understanding of the tools that could be used within coaching. I will focus on the primary coaching tool for the purposes of this example. This primary tool would be the tool that could be used in the workplace as part of the VBL model.

The GROW tool was designed by Sir John Whitmore and serves as the primary tool to set goals and develop an action plan. Whilst it is most commonly used in the context of one-on-one coaching, it can be employed in the context of personal goal setting and workplace goal setting too. The GROW tool is essentially a framework for directing effective questions about the goal and its achievement. It can be used in conjunction with other coaching and management tools. It consists of four stages:

Goal: This stage involves us focusing our attention solely on the outcome or performance goal that we ultimately desire. Here it is important that we employ all the tools and guidelines applicable to goals and the goal setting process. The outcome of this stage should be a goal that is both clearly and precisely defined – accepting of course that it may well change in the future.

The type of questions we might ask ourselves at this stage

---

[12] Coaching – the Ugly Truth possible title for the next book?

could include "what do I want to achieve", "how might I make this goal more specific", "how can I make this goal measurable" and "do I really think that my goal is achievable by me through my own efforts"? We might also ask ourselves, "are there any sub-goals that I might include as milestones to reaching my goal" and "when do I want to have achieved my goal by"?

In order to get the right goal we have to employ SMART. I have seen too often goals that are not set using SMART and ultimately they fail. This is true of company objectives, if they are not set using SMART then ultimately the company has little chance of achieving them.

Reality: This stage involves us considering our current situation by reflecting upon where we are "now" in relation to our goal. The most important criterion for doing this is objectivity. Often people distort their reality with the opinions, judgments, expectations and beliefs of other people – in addition to those that they undoubtedly hold themselves.

For this reason it is important for us to maintain a degree of detachment and be descriptive rather than evaluative. At the end of this stage it is usually worth checking that the original goal that we made is still valid. Many people find that they need to amend it in light of what they have learned about themselves during the reality stage.

The type of questions we might ask ourselves at this stage could include, "what is my current situation now with respect to my goal", "how close to my goal am I", "what are the reasons for this" and "how do I think achieving my goal will make me think, feel and act in the future"? In terms of our graduate, the reality could be what is your current position in relation to being the CEO? What is your current score in relation to achieving your KPI score for the year?

Options: Having looked at the reality of our current situation, this stage involves us considering the options available in terms of how we might make our goal a reality. It is important to recognize, however, that the purpose of this stage is not so much to find the "right" answer, as it is to create and list as many alternatives as possible.

In doing so, we should continually try to think "outside of the box", whilst reflecting objectively on the relative strengths and weakness of each option, what things we might already have in support of each option, and yet other things we might need. Throughout this stage we have to beware of negative assumptions such as "that option wouldn't work" or "I wouldn't be allowed to do that".

By asking ourselves effective questions, or better still getting other people to ask them of us, we can over-ride this negative and self-limiting tendency and challenge the reality of our situation by asking ourselves "what are the reasons for me thinking this way". Similarly, the "what if" approach often produces yet more options. In this way we might ask ourselves, "what if I had more time" or "what if this wasn't the case". Often, however, we might be unable to see an option that someone else can.

Here, we might ask others, "are there any options that I haven't yet considered?" But having asked the question we must at least be prepared to consider the answer!

Examples of other questions that we might ask during this stage might include "how might I achieve this goal", "how have other people achieved similar goals" and "what other options might I have open to me"? This ends up a list of action points on what you could do, it's not the list of what you will do although it is easy to mix the two up.

Will: Whilst the Options stage is about what we "could" do, the Will stage is about what we "will" do. This is arguably the most important stage because it is the one in which decisions are made and from which action is derived. It is during this stage that we ask ourselves "what option(s) will I choose?"

Having run down our list of options and summarized them, we may well have just one preferred option that we wish to act upon or several that we wish to implement at once. Alternatively, we might prioritize several options on the basis of "if that doesn't work then I'll do this". Once we have made our choice, it is often a good idea to check that our chosen course of action will help us achieve our goal.

It is then essential to commit to our time scale by asking ourselves, "when will I start working towards my goal?" If we have employed the GROW tool properly, committing to our action plan in this way is the natural conclusion to the goal setting process.

I have seen this tool adapted by other consultants, authors and coaches, especially if they are creating their own coaching tools and change the "will" to "way forward". This would be my only gripe on this, as normally the words change but the meaning stays the same, but in the 'way forward' it ends up 'wishy washy', you have just created a really SMART Goal and then right at the end the action plan is not as specific as it could be, if the word 'will' is used.

Going back to the example questions that I mentioned earlier in this chapter, I can now place them into examples of GROW Tool questions as follows:

Goal Questions:

What do you want to achieve?
What is important to you right now?
What would you like to get from the next 30 minutes?
What areas do you want to work on?
Describe your perfect world
What do you want to achieve as a result of this session?

Reality Questions:

Where are you now in relation to your goal?
On a scale of 1 -10 where are you?
What has contributed to your success so far?
What skills/knowledge/attributes do you have?
What progress have you made so far?
What is working well right now?

Option Questions:

What are your options?
How have you tackled this/or had similar situation before?
What could you do differently?
Who do you know who has encountered a similar situation?
If anything was possible what would you do?
What else?

Will Questions:

Which options work best for you?
What one small step are you going to take now?
What actions will you take?
When are you going to start?
Who will help you?
How will you know you have been successful?
How will you ensure that you do it?
On a scale of 1 -10 how committed /motivated are you to doing it?

A friend of mine wrote a technical book on training management[13] and they incorporated this tool into a number of elements within the system that they had created, which proves that it can be adapted and used outside of the context of coaching. It can be used as easily in other forms of business and management to illicit results. This is an example of why GROW has ended up being labelled the primary coaching tool.

Motivation

It would be no good if an individual's motivation was lacking or they were ill equipped to motivate themselves. Motivation is the driving force behind burning ambition, determination and commitment. It is also one of the most difficult areas of psychology to understand.

Most psychological theories concentrate on either the personal or situational factors that account for differences in motivation. But there are fundamental principles that

---

[13] Cording, Vincent E, (2014), *Training Management – The Six Stage Training Model*, Amazon

invariably hold true, irrespective of the other ways in which we might consider motivation, that provide powerful insights into why people do the things they do and why, and sometimes, they don't do the things that perhaps they know they should.

Getting them to be highly motivated was key, and the secret to attaining motivation is by the use of goal setting, and going through the process explained earlier. If this is in place then they have to be motivated to get the results. You cannot progress to a performance stage if they haven't generated the responsibility. This reinforces the fact that you cannot move onto the next stage without the prior one in place.

Attitude

All of the above had to be linked with a person's attitude, they have to have the right one don't they? On a day-to-day basis, people and organizations enter situations, meet people and encounter things that have the potential to impact upon our attitude, with both positive and negative. An understanding of attitude is therefore important because how we think determines how we feel, how we feel determines what we do, and what we do ultimately determines our performance.

In this way, attitude is central to such things as optimism and a person's state of mind. It is therefore important to maintain a positive mental attitude in order to maximize performance, which you can see links back to the definition of coaching that we discussed earlier. It has to be linked to get the performance.

By being around positive people, watching motivational programs and reading positive books, whether they be personal development texts, or inspirational biographies or simply good novels, it is possible to acquire a positive attitude through vicarious or social learning.

By identifying these things and subjecting ourselves to them on a regular basis we can condition ourselves accordingly. We can learn, adopt and become positive people or organizations, and the more positive we are the more we are likely to achieve positive results.

Practical Exercise

Now that I have explained in essence the "what and how" of coaching, as a leadership tool within VBL, that I would go on to use and develop, let's try a little practice. For this you will need a piece of paper, pen or pencil, A4 size will be the most suitable for this. This will confirm that what you have been reading has worked and serves as a form of training transfer. I will refer back to this exercise later in the book.

I want you to draw a large rectangle to the left side of the piece of paper but leave a big enough gap on the right side so that you can place in some notes. At the top of the paper, towards the left and above the rectangle, I want you to write the word Goal.

Now that we have this in place I want you to think of a specific career goal that you want to achieve: it could be an appointment, or something as achieving a particular KPI at work. I want you then to apply SMART to the goal that you have written. Does it stand up to applying SMART? If it does then great, if not, you need to change the Goal so that you can achieve the SMART principles.

At the bottom left below the rectangle I want you to write Reality, and place in where you are now in relation to the goal that you have written. For example, if the goal was an appointment or promotion the reality could be your present position, if it was a KPI, the reality could be the KPI current score in relation to the score that you want to achieve (Goal).

You now have the "where you want to be", and the "where you are". Now place on the right towards the top the word Options, and I want you to produce a list of everything that you could do in order to achieve the goal, there is no right or wrong for this, but just keep writing everything that you can think of to achieve the goal.

Now that you have your options written down I want you to analyze what you have written down and pick one the you Will do, one point from the list that you have written down and that you Will do. I am going to hold you to this, that your committing to do that one thing.

If you then look at the rectangle that you have drawn, you could place on that one task that you will do in the form of a step, and once you have completed that step you have moved closer towards achieving that goal. Imagine you had produced all the steps required and achieved them, then you would have achieved the goal.

I will check back later to see how you have gotten on with your exercise.

The Leadership Consultant

I was now armed with the experience, new technical skills, attitude and motivation to go out and to be the finished article as a Leadership Consultant, or so I thought. I had gone out and researched leadership and coaching with the most up to date skills. I had this new outlook on leadership, and life in general, and it was as if I had been the 'bad cop' and now it was the time to be the "good cop", a total transformation.

I had my leadership golf bag, which was equipped with the a range of leadership clubs, and was ready to be unleashed on the unsuspecting corporate world. I was going to make all the difference to all the organizations that I came into contact with.

Here then was the problem. I found that I now needed empirical evidence that this new knowledge and skills would work. How would I get an organization to change or adopt these new methods or methodology if there was no evidence that it worked. How could I prove that using the VBL model would get results?

There was a lot of academic theory that suggested that it would, and I truly believed it would, but it in reality no one was talking about it working in the work place. What I needed was an organization that could act as my 'guinea pigs' in a controlled environment where I could control the outcome and get results and performance through adopting VBL.

Chapter 5 – The Guinea Pig

Choosing the Organization?

How hard could it be to find an organization that would allow me to play with their leadership frame work? This would be easy, I thought, as all organizations would be falling over backwards to have me "fix" their respective leadership, wouldn't they?

Looking for an organization that is willing to allow you to mess with their leadership is not as easy as it sounds. How for example can you suggest to them that here is this great way of getting results linked to leadership, and I can get you those results, but I don't have any evidence that it works?

This was not that easy. I discovered that you can't just walk into an organization and announce that you're here to fix their leadership, it is very much a case of diplomatic tight rope. Imagine now you say to someone: I'm here to change your model of leadership. The first thing that they traditionally say is "what's wrong with my leadership?"

Once you are through the door you then have the battle which usually goes like: Who are you? How much? Have you done this before?? Who are else are currently using this leadership model at the moment? Show me where this has worked in the past.

If you come from a academic or educational institution you are going to have the resources to make things work, however, in these types of organization then they tend to be heavily based in the academic world or designed off the shelf to make money and not customized for the specific individuals or companies needs.

Academic organizations traditionally base results on theory and are rarely commissioned to conduct large scale leadership research studies in industry. If they did we would all be reading the Oxford University Model of leadership and adopting it accordingly. I didn't have any of these resources at the time, it was just me. I had come from having lots of resources at the leadership school, to the only resource was me. Before I had had the backing of the organization that I had worked in which gave me a form of credibility.

This then was not going to be as easy as I initially thought to find the right company that would allow me in and full autonomy. I spent time looking for the right organization and was up against it, as lots of doors were shut in my face. Looking back, these doors that were shut in my face were shut for all the right reasons.

They were protecting their interests, and as such safe guarding themselves. Also, because I had worked in one organization for the majority of my working life. I had very little commercial experience. This was an eye opener for me. I knew I needed to get commercial experience, but how could I get it if doors were constantly shut in my face. I then had what we call a piece of pure "luck".

If I was preaching leadership I would say of course this was not luck or chance it was because I stayed positive and I had made it happen with the right kind of motivation and attitude. I had not seen the failure in the doors being shut, but the fact that I saw one door shutting was another opportunity to open a new door.

The Organization

I was speaking to a friend who I had known for a long time and they were part of a large UK Government training organization that was responsible for taking new employees through a performance based training programme over a period of fourteen weeks. The trainees in this programme had to pass a number of performance tests throughout the training, and if successful they were then allocated a place in the main organization.

If they had failed any of the performance tests they were then re-tested, and if still unsuccessful over a period they were either placed back in the programme in another group or asked to leave. Having individuals who did not pass first time, or who were placed back or asked to leave, was having a large impact on the organizations ROI.

My friend was employed as the Training Officer (TO) and was responsible for all matters related to training including the performance of trainees and training standards for all the instructors. The organization had just gone through a period of restructuring and now they were looking at pass rates, as currently they were averaging a 65% first time pass rate for each group.

The TO had been tasked to increase the first time pass rate, and had started to explore different methods of leadership performance, and by chance we found that we were focusing in the same direction, they were looking at something similar to VBL. I was invited to the organization to discuss the possibility of working together. This was just the type of organization that I could get stuck into and prove that this VBL would work.

Why Pass Rates?

I have often been asked this frequently, what is the impact of improving first time pass rates? I have had numerous conversations with clients, and in particular Training Managers, about the significance of improving first time pass rates, even if the company is non-profit they can still have an impact on the budget. I would go on to explain the importance of pass rates as follows:

Let's take an organization that has one hundred employees going through a training development programme that includes a number of performance tests that they have to pass. Each performance test lasts approximately one hour, however the assessor has to spend an hour before a

For one performance test there are one hundred hours for the individuals and a total of three hundred hours for the assessors, making a total of four hundred hours. If the organization has a working day of eight hours that is a total of fifty days in training assessing to assess one performance.

The training organization I was invited to look at had a first time pass rate of 65%, which meant that they had to find another seventeen days of re-assessing. This does not take into consideration any time on any re-training that may be needed. If an hour could be measured in money at the value of 200 the total cost of a second assessment would be $28k.

Imagine that there is one performance test each month, then there is a total re-assessment bill of $336k per year. Remember, this is on only one performance test. Imagine that there are twelve and you can see quickly why increasing the first time pass rates are important to any organization that has this type of performance.

Increasing the pass rate is going to have a direct link with the bottom line or budget, it has too, if trainees are passing first time, there has to be an impact on the training bill, but if more are passing first time it's going to have an impact on the performance of the organization as performance rises so the bottom line will too.

When I have explained this to TOs or heads of HR you

can see the light bulb going on, the spark that they have just understood something for the first time. Improve the construction method of a product and you end up with a better product, a better product normally means you can make more money as there is a marked improvement in quality you can raise the price.

The Meeting

I arrived at the organization and I was immediately impressed by the look and layout. The TO had done a lot of work on establishing the values and getting them cemented into the psyche of the organization. They had been rebranded, and a lot of work had been done getting them as the foundation of all that is underpinned in the company.

I was encouraged as well, as the TO explained that the values were not just words on a piece of paper, they had ensured that each member of staff knew the values and what they meant for the organization as a whole. These values were also passed on to those trainees, so they understood their specific part in them. What was the issue was still raising the first time pass rates and reducing the training bill on re-assessment.

I met with the CEO and VP and I was again impressed with the vision that they both had, which is in tandem with the TO. Both were determined to improve the pass rates, but using the strong core values they had established. The TO was tasked with improving the pass rates; this was to be the main objective for TO. The TO was going to be measured against this performance as part of their KPIs.

As we spoke it was clear that we were all talking the same language and that we were all aligned in our thinking. Now to the problem of first time pass rates. As we discussed the issue the picture for me built, they had a number of trainees that go through a fourteen week program, each trainee had an instructor who also acted as the assessor and the ratio is approx 1:8.

The organization had some excellent instructors, some average instructors and some that were acceptable. All instructors are given to the organization from the UK Government and they were not involved in that selection process, so they had no say in which instructors they got. They had to work with what they had. Some of the instructors were achieving really high pass rates and some not so high.

They wanted to know how they could improve the pass rates as they had tried all they could with the trainees and had looked into all kinds of initiatives to provide incentives for the trainees, but to no avail, they still were not making an improvement on the first time pass rates.

As we are talking it suddenly hit me: the issue was not with the trainees, the issue was with the instructors. The trainee is just a product going through a fourteen week conveyer belt. The product is only as good as the tools making it, in this case the instructor, and some products were made really well, some not so good, and others were bordering on faulty.

They had no control over the instructors that they got sent to them, but they could control what happened to them when they had them. If they could develop the tool

(Instructor), then, at the end of the fourteen weeks they would have a better product and the pass rate will have had to increase.

The CEO, VP and TO all agreed and I now I had my first organization.

The Instructor Leadership Plan

I was allowed to work with one team in the organization but not allowed to change course content, or test procedures; I had boundaries placed on me, so that the trainees would not be disadvantaged. This also works from an academic point of view as by working with just one test group I could have a number of control groups that I could bench mark against. It makes sense to control the impact, and working with just one group I created a pilot plan.

I had looked at the training that all the instructors received prior to them taking up the role of instructor within the organization, and all had been on a training course on how to teach at some point. What varied was the course that the instructors had been on to gain their respective training qualification.

For some the course had been over seven weeks in duration, and for others only two weeks. What they were missing was a common start point and additional skill set to maximize performance from the trainees. I decided to conduct an intervention on the instructors before and during the fourteen week course.

The intervention consisted of me working a level up from

the instructors, and was in the form of a series of workshops. The workshops involved teaching the theoretical and applied aspects of the VBL model, coaching, and when and how to use them within the intervention. What I was using was the literature from the leadership and coaching chapters. All of the training and workshops were essentially taken from, this based in the VBL model.

The intervention was focused on the models that help bridge the gap between theory and practice. The models that were used primarily focused in on the concept of people performance; models are used as an integrated pragmatic theory of performance that transforms the art of communication into the science of results.

As such, it provided a robust framework with which to consult, train, coach and mentor people in their performance, and it offered a proven learning system with which to develop emotional intelligence alongside technical competence, invest in people as well as performance, and realize organizational objectives whilst facilitating personal growth.

I gave the instructors a series of performance models that they could use to elicit results from their trainees. In most instances, once the model had been looked at they would then use the GROW Tool to help set the realistic objectives for each respective trainee. This kept it as easy as possible for each instructor, for as long as they were competent in the GROW tool they knew they would be able to get results.

One of the key elements in this success was going to be

the TO. I worked with them on a 1-1 basis, and passed on all of the skills that I had in order for them to be able to take over when my period of consultation was over. This 1-1 was important with the TO as during the procedure of the plan, I was going to conduct 1-1s with the instructors, but they would need to feel confident in the management to take over this role when I left. The TO was the ideal person to take this on. This was important to me to ensure that the organization could stand on its own two feet when I had left.

Procedure

During the build up to the trainees arriving, the instructors had a week of induction beforehand. The nature of the week for the instructors was to develop the skills that were to be used throughout and to practice them. This week was my time to impart the knowledge and skills that had been acquired and to get the instructors to take responsibility for their actions in the upcoming training of trainees.

The training was given in two stages, and stage one was the initial training that was given to the instructors as explained above. They then produced their own development plan based on their own individual improvement target that was needed in order to raise the first time pass rates.

Stage two was the support that was given to the instructors throughout the training period to the trainees. This was primarily conducted by me to the instructors in the form of coaching periods throughout to help them apply the new skills that they were employing, and to be on hand to give feedback, advice and mentoring as requested. Getting them to set goals, use effective questions, give constructive feedback and use observation skills were encouraged throughout.

This stage enabled training transfer to take place; it also meant that the instructors had a safety net to fall back on. This meant that the trainees always had confidence in the instructors and the instructors had confidence in the fact that I was there if required, if they needed additional support.

This training transfer was the key element in ensuring that this confidence was in place. It all linked back to the process and it enabled the facilitation of performance. Without the training transfer taking place the performance would not have been able to take place.

Traditionally, the instructors had been left to just get on with it, now they were being coached themselves on their own performance, and as they developed then they could see the results in their trainees. What I had been doing was following the process that I outlined earlier of Raising Awareness, Generating Responsibility and Facilitating Performance, which were then measured in the form of first time pass rates.

Results

At the end of the fourteen week training for the trainees, looking at the results was the most important aspect for the management, who – you will remember had been achieving a 65% first time pass rates prior to the intervention. At the end of this training the group achieved a 87% first time pass rate[14], an increase of 22%, but what does that mean in real terms though?

If we go back to our original analogy of pass rates, focusing on one hundred students, then applying the first time pass rate of 87% against 65%, this would mean a real time saving of $17.6k per month and over a year $211.2k could be saved in re-assessing. This was a saving in the training bill to the organization, if they could replicate the results across the organization.

This saving was purely based on improving first time pass rates. If these results could be replicated across the origination, and in each department, then the scope for performance increase would be great.

Imagine now that these results could be replicated, then the level of performance in this organization would be staggering. If this was a profit organization and the results represented improvements to the bottom line. Any company would want to implement this form of leadership, wouldn't they?

The organization benefited from having a strong management team in place, and a TO that was willing to develop, and had the same attributes that were outlined in the VBL model. It is interesting to note that the TO was promoted, and took on a more strategic role, and they are currently continuing to ensure that performance is gained

---

[14] Results are available through an academic paper by the author through Porstsmouth University in the UK

through the same methodology. Their replacement received a TTT package to ensure that the philosophy was 'this isn't new, this is something that we just do.' This ensured that the VBL system continued and is currently still in place.

Loaded Results

The issue for the results was of course that they were loaded in my favour. Here was an organization that was lead by individuals who set the right example, and were willing to change, there were no barriers to the intervention, and they welcomed it.

The organization was used to performance driven goals and they adapted quickly. The test instructors had been chosen as they were the most likely to get results and adopt the new methods. They were seen as the champions of change.

The organization had come to me, and wanted to change. The interesting thing is that at the end of the intervention a train the trainer was conducted with a number of selected individuals across the company, that then went and conducted similar interventions on other groups of instructors. What resulted in this organization over a two year period, was that they were achieving consistently over 85% first time pass rates and in some instances over 90%.

As a result of this success I was able to replicate it across a number of similar organizations with similar results. The reason I was able to get into other similar organizations, and not have the door closed on me, was that I had now proven that VBL worked.

I was now able to measure the improvement of performance that could be linked to the bottom line, and here then was the empirical evidence that it would work. The organizations that I went on to work with, were all high performance in nature, and all were willing to change. This change had been led from the top down.

What would happen if I came up against an organization that was none of the above?

Chapter 6 – Getting it all Wrong

Setting the Scene

Traditionally at this stage, when you may have read a leadership, management, coaching, self help or any form of book from the business section, as an example, the author would go on to explain all the positive results that they had subsequently gone on to achieve. They would explain that great things await you by following the proven steps of success that were mentioned throughout their book.

I could now go on to do that, I have explained how great results were achieved in the previous chapter, it's would be just a case of role modelling what went well and replicating those actions.

Of course if it was only as simple as that, we would all be at the top, we would all be leaders of industry, we would all be the CEO, we would all be instant success stories that those self help books suggest you could be. How many books have you read where the author explains where it has gone wrong for them, where it hasn't worked?

Surely there must be instances of individuals who have not got the results that they were looking for, or the results weren't all positive? Where are the books on getting it all wrong? To that end there are lots of books on leadership, but in order to be a leader we need followers, where are the books on followship? If leadership is important then followship must be equally as important.

In the real world, sometimes, we don't get the results we are looking for, sometimes we have to learn from our own performance and behaviour. This had happened to me in the past. I had a project in a large organization that didn't go to plan, but on paper it looked like the ideal project to further enhance the VBL that I had been developing, and it has now cemented a number of procedures and values that I now stick too when selecting new clients to work with as a result of getting it all wrong. Some individuals would call this experience failure, but for me, it was a developmental experience in my performance as a consultant.

The Organization

I had been approached by an organization, which wasn't one that I would normally have worked with, as it was outside my sphere of expertise. So far I had been dealing with high performance Government or Semi Government organizations dealing with performance issues that were measured against results and could be easily identified.

This organization was coming out of a period of restructuring, and were suffering in their bottom line as a result of a recent economic downturn. They wanted to improve their bottom line, and one way that they were looking to do that, was improving their top talent to spread a culture of performance. They were looking to introduce a specific leadership programme to accomplish this.

This sounded reasonable at this stage, and investing in the future of its employees seemed to me that they were moving in the right direction. Especially by linking it to the development of top talent.

The organization explained that they had in the past performed well on the targets that it needed, and at one stage had been the lead within their respective field. However, they were now experiencing strong competition from other growing, similar companies. The main performance came from the senior management and a number of high performing sales individuals.

The large amount of first line managers and subordinates would have no real impact to the bottom line. The senior management and high performing sales people were headhunted into the organization, and not groomed from within.

This explanation was important as the company suggested that they didn't really believe in the majority of their own workforce, they saw the development of the top talent as the key to success. This could be seen by the majority, that they may feel that they were not valued by the organization.

They saw the development in only the top talent, and not in the rest of the organization. This should have set off some alarm bells at this stage, as ideally they should have seen the importance in their whole workforce development, and not just a select few.

The First Meeting

They had arranged for me to meet the team who were going to be responsible for the introduction of this leadership program. The first thing that I noticed was that they had already brought in an outside consultant to lead this project. I was introduced to this individual and straight away, noticed that this could prove a little difficult as they had hired an external consultant to lead this and then they were now speaking to me to run the project? I was consulting the consultant.

It was then explained that they wanted their top talent to be able to coach their respective teams within the leadership framework, and improve results. Although they had eluded that they didn't recognize the part the workforce played, by getting a leadership framework in place through their top talent it would have the effect of developing the workforce indirectly as they would have to have an impact on those around them and cascading the effect of the leadership framework. Not ideal but still workable within the VBL model.

If I wanted the business, then I was asked to design a proposal to enable their vision of leadership to happen. I was told I was to answer to the outside consultant on all matters. Any questions or issues that I may have, I was only to speak to them. At the time this sounded normal to me as I had heard of sub contracting, as it happens all the time in industry, but I had not heard it happen in this field unless the parties had previously worked together, or had formed partnerships.

It was also the first time that I was asked for a detailed proposal, that I was asked to put together to justify the expense. It seemed that they were only interested in the money and not the outcomes. Of course the money was important, but it shouldn't be the main factor, and the consultant explained that I was also to have nothing to do with the main company, everything had to go through them.

I later found out that they did this with a number of parties and then played us off against one another to get the lowest price. This wasn't about outcomes of the project but how much it was going to cost them. It was at this stage that I should have walked away. However, I decided to submit the proposal.

The Proposal

I worked on a detailed proposal, adopting very similar methods to those I had seen used in previous companies, that had got the required success. I had stressed the autonomy to work in the organization, and help those individuals to gain the results specific to the project elements.

I researched the company and used their values to base the proposal around fitting in with the VBL model, as their values had just been redesigned as part of their restructuring process. It followed the general format that had worked for other consultants that I had known in the past, so I submitted it to the consultant.

The consultant then sent a detailed reply back saying that I couldn't do what I wanted to do as this was what they were employed to do, and that they would deal with any individual 1-1 sessions that might take place, and take the lead where appropriate. They explained that I would deliver the intervention to the group and that they would take care of the rest.

That's all I would be employed to do, for this part. In essence, I was bought in to conduct an off the shelf programme to fit in with what the consultant had designed for the top talent of the company. The training transfer would be looked after by them as they were experts in this field of leadership. At this stage all seemed plausible. In essence. I was just a facilitator delivering a piece of instruction within leadership to the top talent.

The consultant explained, that they had a lot of experience in this field and that they were more experienced than me in this type of organization and that they were more suited to deliver the workplace piece to the project. Certainly on paper they were and I thought maybe I could gleam more experience from them to expand my knowledge. I agreed to conduct the training to a number of small groups. Again this was a big mistake, it wasn't too late and I should have walked away…

The Training

The training that I would conduct was going to be based on the VBL model, and then focus on coaching their subordinates for performance, and this would have the desired effect on the organization to increase the performance. The methodology and literature covered in earlier chapters was used. The consultant explained that they would sit in on all training delivery, so that they could "help" if required.

On the morning of the first group, I did the normal meet and greet and gave the brief history of how I had ended up here. This was to establish a base line of credibility and I explained the training that was about to take place. The consultant then stepped in to explain that any questions or advice was to go through them and not me.

Straight away I been made to feel that I was here to just stick a few slides on a PowerPoint, and then allow the consultant to take all the credit. Throughout the training, the consultant would intervene and make their own point on material that I was discussing (more about this later). I had now been employed as a basic instructor, not the consultant that I was brought in for or that they needed.

As I was basing the training on their own company values, I was interested to see how much they knew about them, but it turned out that they had not heard of them, they thought that they had some but had not seen them. I explained to them that if they didn't know their own values how were they going to get the desired behaviour from their subordinates?

This could be replicated for them and the top management. This was something we would look at on the training, and it was surprising as they had only been redesigned. This was an important issue for a number of organizations, because they have excellent designed values, but they have not cascaded them in the company, or they don't understand the behaviour that they want from them. They end up remaining just words on a piece of paper.

At the first break the consultant came to see me and said that they had never seen anything like what I was delivering and could they if they sat in all the workshops get a certificate the same as the individuals on the course? Here was the consultant that was employed to conduct this project, that was neither qualified or had the right experience to lead it.

They asked that we keep this between the two of us, as if the organization found out they would lose their contract. Here then was the consultant who was proving to be extremely difficult for me on this project, not qualified to conduct the training transfer, asking me to help them so that they didn't look bad, take the credit for my work and undermine me at all levels, there was nothing wrong with that? I agreed to help them. It wasn't too late to walk away.

This is where my values had kicked in, and I could not let this individual fail, I had to help them as if the consultant was allowed to fail, then this would have a direct impact on the students on the program. They could not be disadvantaged due to this shortcoming, after all it wasn't their fault.

As the training continued it became clear that the students were really enjoying the programme and they clearly understood the theory. They were looking forward to taking the theory into the workplace. This was going to be really interesting as this is where I stopped and the consultant took over. This was now really important to the learners, especially in the workplace, as this is where the performance was to take place including the training transfer.

I had gotten to know some of the group really well, and had developed deep rapport with them, and I was able to ask about any other development programme that they would be undertaking. They explained to me that this was just one course that they are taking as part of the consultants development plan for their top talent program. They were just taking part in back to back programs and felt overloaded in training programs.

The Consultant Development Plan

I found out that my training was just a part of a development plan that the other consultant has arranged for this top pool of senior managers. Now this is nothing new as most top talent have development plans that are linked to succession planning amongst other things. This is often best practice in large companies.

The group explained to me that they were doing back to back programs and that all of their time was taken up with conducting courses. I asked them if they were doing any other leadership programs, and it turned out that they were to undertake a week's intense leadership programme from a very well known organization at a large cost to the company. This sounded great, and certainly a course from this organization compared to me, would look better on the CV than mine. Indeed, I would have liked to have been a student on this.

I asked the students what was the outcome for all of these projects? What was linking them all together? How was the performance going to be measured? They explained to me that they felt that they were just doing courses for the sake of doing courses. This was an important perception from the students as they believed that they were only doing these courses as paper exercise, and they would only get the performance that reflected that perception.

I thought that I better have a conversation with the consultant as this was going to have an impact on the desired effect of the training that I was delivering.

The consultant explained to me that this was not my concern and that I should just focus on the delivery of my programme. I asked the consultant what was their role in this development plan. As they explained it to me, it dawned on me that they were not acting in the role of a consultant, they were just a programme coordinator to bring a number of programmes together, and facilitate their delivery.

I asked them how they were going to be able to conduct the training transfer that I had explained needed to be done in the proposal, as this was this was more important than the delivery to illicit the performance increase. I got back the reply "not my concern", this is what they were contracted to do.

Training Transfer

The programme that I had created had come with accreditation based on the consultant being able to conduct the training transfer within the organization, which was part of the accreditation process, the 1-1 sessions with each student. Now, bearing in mind that the consultant was neither current nor competent, having had to get this from me, this was now developing into a disaster for this program. Especially as what I had done was to allow the consultant to gain accreditation through the back door for themselves, and them not being able to conduct these 1-1 sessions.

The consultant was not able to conduct the training transfer; the contract was set up in a way for me not to be able to do this as the consultant was to undertake this role. This was having huge complications on the accreditation and, more importantly, on the group, as they were not receiving 1-1 that they needed to get the accreditation that they required.

I was now at a crossroads as the organization was not getting the results, the accreditation was failing as I had not been allowed to conduct this on the basis that the consultant was covering this. The consultant was now blaming me for all of the failings of the individuals and lack of performance results. All due to the fact that training transfer had not been allowed to take place as the consultant had set it up to fail. Due to the way that the consultant had set the contract up I was unable to conduct the 1-1 sessions with each student.

The Hardest Decision

This was a stalemate, and the only solution that was left to me was to explain to the organization top management about the consultant and my point of view and the impact it was having on the students. The problem with this was that there had been no involvement from them. They were not interested in any development at all; they were only interested in being see to be taking an interest. They were completely disengaged from the programme.

There was an evident gap in them and the management beneath them. If they weren't interested then the behaviour that they were getting across the organization was easy to see why.

The organization was in a complete mess, and explaining the shortcomings of this consultant was not going to solve the issues within it.

I decided to walkway having ensured that the group still received the outcome of the proposal and that all objectives were covered. They just weren't going to be covered by me. I made sure that another consultant was brought in to cover any subsequent work or delivery to ensure that the students weren't disadvantaged, but it came to that stage where I had to walk away.

Walking Away

Walking away from this organization remained with me for a long time afterwards, it certainly dented my reputation, and all I had to do was come clean about the consultant and all would have been ok. But why didn't I? This was another lesson in my own development, and when I reflect on this organization it's easy to see where the mistakes took place and what could have been done to rectify them.

But I look back at that first meeting and I should have just said no. I was riding this crest of success and thought that it would be easy. I thought that I could achieve anything.

The truth is do any of us like to admit that we can't do something. Now, if you go back to all of the leadership courses and self help books this programme should have succeeded and the results would have come. But here is a lesson in real life. We don't always get the results that we were expecting. The secret is not accepting this as failure but feedback for the future. I could not let this result affect me, I had to use it to ensure that it did not happen in the future.

I wonder how many of us have experienced the types of results in the past, or are going to experience them in the future?

Case Study

I now use my own experience of this organization as a case study that I have developed to use in certain programmes. I am often reminded in what Thomas Edison said when asked about failing so many times inventing the light bulb: he suggested that he had not failed, only discovered 9'999 ways not to create a light bulb.

I have now developed as a result of this experience a detailed case study that I use in developing consultants, especially, as it was real life, then the consultants can relate to it as it is not something that was created. This negative outcome was something that could be used as a positive development tool for future consultants.

Chapter 7 – Success

Initial Reflection

After experiencing success and failure I decided to conduct reflection on what I had achieved so far, and take stock of what could I learn from both success and the things that had not gone to plan? Certainly I gained some credible results and had been successful for the most part. On the other hand I had almost got caught up in my own success.

As a result of all of this experience, what could I draw upon, and how could I use this for the future? What could I learn from this and how could I use these experiences to help develop myself in order to better facilitate performance from others?

Here's a question for you: have you ever tried to conduct

any form of reflection? What does reflection look like? Do you just talk about it, or do you write it down? I had started to ponder on how to reflect, and I was now reflecting on reflection. If you think about it, have you ever been on a reflection course?

Most courses that you may have been on, normally have elements of reflection built into the design, but rarely are we taught how to reflect. This is was something that I had built into my programmes, and interventions, but paid more of a lip service activity than something detailed. Still, here I was having achieved success and failure, so it was time that I took reflection seriously.

I had seen a lot of course material over the years that has had reflection built into it, but the trainer or facilitator were ill equipped to get learners to reflect, and this was because they too had little understanding of the benefits of reflection. This was also true of consultants working with companies: how did they also get the organization to reflect? Looking at myself, it was something that I would go through with individuals or organizations, but just as a paper exercise.

I had decided that I needed to brainstorm all that I had done in the past, and I acquired a very large white board that I could write all over, for my reflection exercise. I just started writing all over the board, thinking about all that I had done, and not done.

What I found is that once I started it just came pouring out. I had often heard of people pouring their feelings out and once they start, it's like a tidal wave of emotions that just flood out. This was the same for me on the white board, all of my reflections on past events were poured onto that white board.

The White Board

The white board now looked like a collage of my achievements, good and bad, things I did well, things I had done not so well. I took a couple of days using the white board, coming back to it and adding more. I took a break of two days and when I came back to look at the board it struck me how it looked, I had created a visual representation that when I looked at I could see all my areas for development. It was as if it was taking on an identity of its own.

I looked at the board and these areas of reflection, and in particular the areas where I noticed that I needed personal development. I noticed that I could place on top of these areas the GROW Tool, I could use this as a personal development tool. By conducting this reflection exercise I had now created a powerful tool to help my own personal development.

The organization that had gone wrong was mentioned several times, and this was where many of my areas of development seemed to be based. I found myself suggesting to myself, that on this journey it seemed that it is still easy to focus on the negative and not the positive.

It was interesting that I had created my own GROW in relation to where I was and where I wanted to be for my own personal development. All I needed now, was the options and will to get there.

By producing this GROW on my own reflection it enabled me to produce the required steps to develop and overcome my shortcomings, that had led to negative outcomes, it enabled me to be able to turn these into positive outcomes and to be in a position to handle these type of obstacles if the appeared in the future.

I was able to use them to facilitate positive performance by driving my reality towards my goal. I use this GROW as a reference document still today, and monitor and amend as my development grows.

There are many ways in which to conduct reflection, but I discovered for myself the power of reflection, and how important it is. We all need to find our own way of reflection that works best for ourselves, what is your White Board?

The Commercial Company

After taking time reflecting and developing myself I was invited to a large commercial company to look at development of its in-house managers. Of course the first thing I looked for, was: had they hired an external consultant?

The company had a number of managers that they needed to develop, in order to facilitate an expansion program; they wanted to develop the leadership of each manager, and to ensure that there were positive results as an outcome of the expansion. They also wanted to ensure that there was commonality amongst the managers within the leadership that was adopted.

This development plan had been created by the top management, as they knew that they needed this to work to ensure the success of the expansion, they had also just gone through a rebranding exercise, and strong values had been developed.

Having looked at the organization it had similarities to the organization that had gone wrong, however, this time right from the beginning I was able to ensure that measures were in place to safeguard the intervention that I would be responsible for. These measures, that were in place, were part of my development as a result from my reflection process that I had gone through.

A leadership intervention was designed around the development of their corporate values linked to the individual performance needs of the managers using the VBL model. This was accomplished once the theory had been delivered by creating workplace individual development plans, that were customized for each manager.

This ensured that the training transfer took place, and that the individual manager needs for development and performance were catered for. This was done using the same methods outlined in the previous chapters.

The top management allowed me the freedom to coach the individual managers as required. The individual managers, as the programme progressed, started to gain strong performance results, and noticed significant gains in their respective workforce.

The top management were impressed with this, and asked

for a presentation on how this could be placed across the organization with the junior managers and subordinates. This was the management noticing the results and now looking to replicate them across the company.

I presented to the organization a holistic top to bottom framework that could be used across the organization, using the managers that had already gone through the programme, and with a short train the trainer programme. This could be rolled this out with minimal financial cost.

The top management loved idea, as they could see the resulting increase in performance would have an impact on the expansion programme, and the financial saving helped too. As for me, I was consulting myself out of a job, which was proof of the success of the intervention, that they no longer needed me. How many times have you seen the external consultant hanging on, not wanting to leave the company. Success for me in this instance is seeing the company standing on its own two feet.

They had really bought into the idea, and rolled the programme out after the short train the trainer programme; interestingly though, the programme was rolled out to the company at middle manager and below, the top management was deemed not to need this as they were already competent.

As I left the company, although it may seem that the top management had done 'do as I say not as I do', this was not the case, there had been enough of a cultural change to affect the organization, and although the top management had not been involved in the programme, a sort of osmosis had taken place organically. They were now adopting behaviours from the values that they had commissioned, and the top management were having to change because of the results that were happening below them - Success.

The Government Organization

One of the major achievements that took place later was when I worked with an government organization based on one of their promotion programmes. I was asked to assist in the development of a programme for managers who had been selected for promotion to their top management. The managers had already gained the promotion and this programme was going to be conducted before taking up their new roles, designed at a strategic level.

Having gleamed all of this experience I designed the suggested programme, which mixed in the VBL that I had developed to fit with their specific needs. The programme was based on the early leadership performance with coaching as the main focus that i had conducted at the leadership school.

I had now come full circle, and the leadership had evolved and been adapted but the outcome had stayed the same.

What struck me about this programme was that it was being conducted with a number of individuals that I had worked with over the last 18 years, and as I had visited elements the programme being delivered by these individuals, I noticed that they were using methods that I had seen developed and cultivated.

What they had done was to take that knowledge from me

and adapt it, and they changed it to suit their own needs and were achieving fantastic results within this program. Some of the consultants that I had been fortunate to have worked with in the past had gone on to develop their own form of leadership and were taking it to a new level of performance.

They had adapted it and modified it to suit this company's needs, I had gone from the teacher to the student. This was fascinating, and it ignited my passion once again within leadership, demonstrating that just when you think you are there, there is always something new that we can learn. This never fails to surprise me when it happens.

For me this government organization was the culmination of my leadership journey, to see this in action was the most heart-warming feedback that I could receive. It had made the leadership journey worthwhile. It has to be stressed that because the consultants had taken this and adapted it for themselves the students on the promotion programme were fully engaged.

They readily took the programme back to the workplace, and they took that responsibility to ensure that training transfer was taking place. They were actively seeking new knowledge and skills from the consultants that they could then use to develop themselves further.

The great thing about this is the fact that they had all gained promotion prior to the programme, the reason that they were doing this was for the common goals of the organization, underpinned by a deep understanding of the values. Their performance was linked to this and the consultants' behaviour. You could see the learning taking place, it had become a truly empowered organization.

Success

To me this was what it had all been for, this was what the word success meant, you could not put a price on it, but at that moment it time that is what success looked like. All of the theories, all of the modelling, all of the development of the leadership had come right in this one organization.

The results were truly remarkable too, certainly they were used to gaining great results, but this had previously been done for them, this time they had done it by themselves, for themselves. The results that they were getting were performance driven, that were underpinned by a strong leadership framework that had been created by themselves.

Speaking to my fellow consultants who were also a part of this project, they also concurred that this was by far one of the most rewarding programmes that they had also been on.

They commented on the fact that the learners were responsive and that the results and feedback that they were getting was very good. They also mentioned that this was due to the influence that I had had, I pointed it out to them that it was nothing to do with me, they had done it for themselves, alongside the students.

Chapter 8 – The Secret

The Journey

Coming to the end of my leadership journey I realise that I have had time to reflect on what went well and the areas that didn't go to well. From the point of view within leadership I have contextualized leadership development through the different roles that I have had and I have discovered that it is me that is in charge of my own leadership destiny, it's hard to imagine that when I first started all those years ago that I would end up here.

If you would have asked me to predict that I would be operating at the highest levels in industry, specializing in leadership, I would have said that you were insane at that time.

Life throws us challenges and asks us to ask those difficult questions, how we answer them is important in all our journeys. I look sometimes at some of the people that I have come across, and look at them now, and they have gone on to have the most fantastic careers, often far surpassing that of mine. It gives me the most reward seeing them realize their potential: isn't it, after all, what we teachers do?

Do we hold people back or do we allow them to grow? This goes with those organizations that I have been fortunate to have worked with. Even when it went all wrong there were still positive outcomes. Take the Anti-Coach as an example, they too have had a role to play.

Whatever Happened to the Anti-Coach?

Whatever happened to the Anti-Coach? I mentioned in chapter one? I still know of this individual, as we move in the same social circles, and it's interesting to note that the anti-coach is a living cliché or metaphor for "if you do what you have always done, you will get what you have always got." Nearly twenty years have passed and they are still in the same organization, demonstrating the same behaviours. Have their values changed at all?

There is no doubt or question that the individual has been successful, and this success is particularly frustrating for me to observe, as they had gotten this success by being the Ant-Coach. If they had been able to change or adapt I often think what could have been for them?

But in nearly twenty years there has been no real change, the individuals EQ remains almost at the same level, performance is there, but to think, this person had so much performance potential. They could have made such a positive impact and influenced so many because their knowledge and skills were in place, just not linked to their attitude. If you look at their top level of EQ, social skills, it's still in the same place there, has been no development. If there has been no change in the top level, what has happened to the levels that we can't see?

They have now become a walking cliché, the individual that others call the dinosaur, the last of a 'dying breed.' It is one of my personal regrets that I was unable to affect them from a behavioural change. They are soon to retire from the government job that they have held, and will have to face the future like the dinosaurs, they will have to change, or face extinction.

Lessons Learnt

For me looking back and explaining what lessons can I draw from the experience, and what could you learn from them is not something that you could put into a detailed list of points. It would be great to create a twelve step leadership plan to ensure great success, but as we have discussed this has been done many times before. Which does not guarantee success.

It's not a case of following a step by step program, it has to be looking at each situation that you find yourself in and adapting the leadership to fit. If you try to impose a leadership framework or system onto an organization that is not suited for that type then you will only get partial success.

Think about all those books, that are off the shelf solutions: they are not customized for specific people or organizations. It's going back to the young trainer: what experience do they have in the real world of applying the respective techniques or theories at the highest levels. Think of the leadership golf bag: a good leader has more than one club available for selection.

There is credibility in these techniques and theories but they have to be adapted, they have to be customized. For me the biggest lesson that I have learned is something that we have known for a long time, in that you cannot solve every problem with the same solution.

The biggest lesson is to approach each situation as what it is, something new. We draw on past experiences and knowledge, and then adapt and change to create that specific solution, then and only then can we get the results and performance that are unique to that problem.

The Future

What does the future hold for any us? This is the same for my leadership journey. However, I am now equipped with the fundamental tools, more importantly the life skills to assess the future and make the detailed planning that is required to achieve those next specific leadership goals.

The future is not a place that is unattainable, what I have learnt is that the future is achievable. You can achieve what you want to do as long as you are honest with yourself.

What type of leader do you want to be? How do you want to affect those around you? What results do you want to achieve? What would your model of leadership look like?

Here is the change in language, notice that I have switched from me or I to you, this is no longer about me, this is about what you are going to do? How are you going to achieve your future goals and aspirations? If you could achieve them what would they look like fitting in to the world of leadership?

Challenge

Here is my challenge to you, if you have made it to here, you will have had to have thought about yourself, you will have had to question your own leadership. Therefore I challenge you to go back to the GROW that you did on yourself and reflect, can you make the steps necessary to achieve that particular goal?

Once you know that you can produce a GROW on yourself and that you feel comfortable doing so, here is the challenge: I want you to produce a GROW on the type of leader you want to be or an area of leadership that you want to explore. This is your homework. Do you have the motivation and attitude to give it a go, are you already the great leader? Do you have areas for improvement within your leadership? If you are the finished article that's great, but what can you do to maintain that level?

I'm not going to check your homework, but what have you got to lose? You may be surprised by the results that you come up with. Imagine the feedback you can get on yourself by taking fifteen minutes of your life to examine where you want to be, and how are you going to get there? What is the worst that could happen? Well the worst is you will have wasted fifteen minutes of your life, but imagine the positive change that may occur, imagine being able to influence your own goals, it is your future. I challenge you to give it a go.

The Leadership Secret

The big reveal, the big leadership mystery, by now you will have noticed that it's about simplifying as much as we can in order to get the desired results from leadership. For me it's about not making something it's not, and this is the same for leadership.

It's not magic, there is no dark art to it. People like me, consultants, like to try and make it something special, something only experts can use or do. It's only for those at the top of management, those selected individuals. We like to try and keep it that way as it keeps individuals like me in business. Certainly there is a great living to made as a consultant.

Consultants, trainers and training organizations, as an example, don't want to give it away do they? If they do this it will put them out of business. But this goes against the values of true leadership, it can never be about me, it has to be what is important to the individual or organization.

Even if this puts me out of a job, this would not be seen as failure but as true success as the individual or organization can now stand on their own two feet. This allows the consultants etc. to move on to the next client building on the success that they have just got, continually building that reputation of VBL. This makes sense from the business development side too, as it can be used as a marketing ploy to gleam more business. But let's reinforce the fact that people like me want to make leadership something it's not!

The Ugly Truth

If you haven't turned to this page from the beginning of the book, and you have held back from reading this section, this is the part where after building leadership, taking you on this journey it's time to reveal the big secret of leadership

So here is my big secret to leadership – the ugly truth of leadership that people like me don't want you to know, who are the people like me though? These are all the trainers, coaches, consultants, training companies, consultation companies that are out to make money from you. These are the line managers that are holding you back, the organizational management that don't want to allow growth. The individuals that keep everything to themselves, a little knowledge is power.

This is what they don't want you to know, the ugly truth to leadership is that there is NO SECRET. If you have been paying attention throughout the book you will have been thinking that this makes sense, I could do that, and the truth is you can, of course you can. With a little development and hard work of course you can, I am living proof that yes you can.

You don't need to spend a fortune on expensive programmes that may or may not work, just think about the type of leadership you want to adopt and make it happen yourself. Think about the process we spoke about earlier: what I have been doing is raising your awareness to leadership and generating responsibility in you, the performance is now up to you...

Leadership is all about you, the ugly truth is there is no secret, plain and simple, it is just about you.

References and Reading List

The Point

Normally at the back of the book, tucked away, are the references, which I bet none of you have really read have you? It's true it serves a purpose to support the writing of the book, but what is the point in listing all of them if they serve no real purpose? For me the reading list serves as a "go to" list for anyone interested in taking their underpinning knowledge and developing it further.

This reading list serves as an impartial list of those individuals who have made an impact in leadership and the development of leadership styles as illustrated earlier in the leadership chapter. These offer the current up to date thinking, and some of the most respected individuals in their respective fields.

Throughout the book I have highlighted where applicable those individuals, books and articles I thought would provide an additional source of reading to help the underpinning knowledge. Working within leadership then it also helps to have the academic back up when asked by clients: where does this come from?

Is there any reference we could look to in order to back up what you're saying. Being able to suggest some academic literature is always good when dealing with organizations.

For me, having a library of reference books or knowing where to go to get them is also good, especially when developing new material or looking to give appropriate advice. There is also something rewarding about reading a book or paper.

The list provided is a suggested reading list of some of the books, articles that I have used along the way to enhance my knowledge. They also stand up as points of reference if required. They also point to other directions of investigations too. I am not suggesting to read them all, but have a look through and see if there any that stand out, certainly Whitmore, Goleman, House, Hardy are some individuals that I find personally enjoyable and developmental.

But that is it, they are just a list that I have found useful, they are not the definitive list, just examples of references and books that I have used. Think of my list in the same way that I presented the leadership styles, they are just examples not the examples, use if required but better to have a list and not use it than to want a list of proven leadership material and not have it.

Reading List

Amabile, T.M. (1998). How to kill creativity. *Harvard Business Review, 76(9):* 77-87.

Atwater, L, E. & Yammarino, F, J. (2003). Personal attributes as predictors of superiors and subordinates perceptions of military academy leadership. *Human Relations, 46,* 654 – 668.

Bachkirova, T., & Cox, E. (2004). A bridge over troubled water: bringing together coaching and counselling. *The International Journal of Mentoring and Coaching,* 2.

Baldwin, T, T., Magjuka, R, J., & Loher, B, T. (1991). The perils of participation: effects of choice on training motivation and learning. *Personnel Psychology, 44,* 51–65.

Barling, J., Weber, T., & Kelloway, E, K. (1996). Effects of transformational leadership training on attitudinal and financial outcomes. *Journal of Applied Psychology, 81,* 827-832.

Bass, B.M. (1985). *Leadership and performance beyond expectations.* New York: Free Press.

Bass, B.M., & Avolio, B.J. (1994). *Improving organizational effectiveness through transformational leadership.* Thousand Oaks, CA: Sage.

Bass, B.M., Avolio, B.J., Jung, D., & Berson, Y. (2003). Predicting unit performance by assessing transformational and transactional leadership. *Journal of Applied Psychology*, 88: 207-218.

Butler, R. (1989). *Psychological Preparation of Olympic Boxers.* In Kremer, J., & Crawford, W., (Eds), *The Psychology of Sport: Theory and Practice (pp74-78).* Leicester: British Psychological Society.

Burns, J. M. (2001). *In a teleconference at the Bernard M Bass Festschrift, State University of New York at Binghampton,* New York, 31 May – 1 June 2001.

Boyer, N. (2003). Leaders mentoring leaders: Unveiling role identity in an international online environment. *Mentoring & Tutoring: Partnership in Learning, 11(1),* 25–42.

Bryman, A., & Bell, W. (2007). *Business Research Methods* (2nd ed). New York. Oxford University Press.

Clutterbuck, D. (2007). *Coaching the Team at Work.* London, Nicholas Brealey.

Cooper, D. R, & Shindler, P. S. (2008). *Business Research Methods* (10th ed). Boston. McGraw-Hill.

Callow, N., Smith, J., Hardy, L., Arthur, C., & Hardy, J. (2009). Measurement of Transformational leadership and its relationship with team cohesion and performance level. *Journal of Applied Sport Psychology, 21 (4),* 395 — 412

Colquitt, J, A., LePine, A., & Noe, R, A. (2000). Toward an integrative theory of training motivation: a meta-analytic path analysis of 20 years of research. *Journal of Applied Psychology, 85* (5), 678–707.

Cording, Vincent E, (2014), *Training Management – The Six Stage Training Model*, Amazon

Csoka, L. S., & Fiedler, F. E. (1972). The effect of military leadership training: a test of the contingency model. *Organizational Behaviour and Human Performance, 8 (3)*, 395–

Dvir, T., Eden, D., Avolio, B. J., & Shamir, B. (2002). Impact of transformational leadership on follower development and performance: a field experiment. *Academy of Management Journal, 45(4)*, 735–744.

Ergi, C, P., & Herman, S. (2000). Leadership in the North American environmental Sector: Values, Leadership Styles, and contexts of environmental leaders and their organizations. *Academy of Management Journal, 43*, 571-604.

Ely, K., Boyace, L, A,. Nelson, J, K., Zaccaro, S, J,. Broome, G. & Whyman, W. (2010). Evaluating leadership coaching: A review and integrated framework. *The leadership Quarterly, 21*, 585 – 599.

Festinger, L. (1959). *A Theory of Cognitive Dissonance*. Stanford, CA. Stanford University Press.

Gross, R. (2001). *Psychology: The science of mind and behaviour*. Hodder & Stoughton.

Gallwey, T, W. (1974). *The inner game of tennis*. Random House.

Goleman, D., Boyatzis, R., & Annie McKee. (2002). *The new leaders: transforming the art of leadership into the science of results*, London: Little, Brown.

Hardy, L., Arthur, C., Jones, G., Shariff, A., Munnoch, K., Isaacs, I., & Allsop, A. (2010). "The relationship between transformation leadership behaviours, psychological and training outcomes in elite military recruits". *The Leadership Quarterly, Volume 21, (1),* 20-32.

House, R, J. (1977). *A 1977 theory of charismatic leadership. Leadership: The cutting edge.* Carbondale: Southern Illinois University Press.

House, R, J. (1999). Weber and neo-charismatic leadership paradigm: A response to Beyer. *The Leadership Quaterly, 10,* 563 – 574.

House, R, J. (1996). Path-goal theory of leadership: Lessons, legacy, and a reformulated theory. *The Leadership Quarterly, 7,* 323–352.

House, R, J., & Shamir, B. (1993). *Toward the integration of transformational, charismatic, and visionary theories.* San Diego, CA: Academic Press.

Howell, J, M., & Frost, P, J. (1989). A laboratory study of charismatic leadership. *Organizational Behaviour and Human Decision Processes, 43,* 243–269.

Jowett, S., & Chaundy, V. (2004). An investigation into the impact of coach leadership and coach athlete relationship on group cohesion. *Group Dynamics: Theory, Research and Practice, 8,* 302-311.

Jung, D., & Avolio, B. (2000). Opening the black box: An experimental investigation of the mediating effects of trust and value congruence on transformational and transactional leadership. *Journal of Organizational Behaviour*, 21: 949-964.

Kirkpatrick, D.L., & Kirkpatrick, J.D. (1994). *Evaluating Training Programs*, Berrett-Koehler Publishers

Kram, K, E. (1985). *Mentoring at work.* Glenview, IL: Scott, Foresman and Company.

Maurer, T, J., & Tarulli, B, A. (1994). Investigation of perceived environment, perceived outcome, and person variables in relationship to voluntary development activity by employees. *Journal of Applied Psychology, 79*, 3–14.

McDermott, M., Levenson, A., & Newton, S. (2007). What coaching can and cannot do for your organization. *Human Resource Planning, 30,* 30–37.

Messmer, M. (2003). Building an effective mentoring program. *Strategic Finance, 84(8),* 17–18.

Noe, R, A., & Schmitt, N. (1986). The influence of trainee attitudes on training effectiveness: test of a model. *Personnel Psychology, 39*, 497–523.

Patrick, J. (2006). *Effectiveness of Coaching Techniques in Military Training: Final Report,* Farnborough, QinetiQ Ltd.

Patrick, J., Ahmed, A., Hodgetts, H., Hutchings, P., Morgan, P., Scrase, G., Tombs, M and Watts, H. (2006). *Effectiveness of coaching techniques in military training.* Final Report HC-05-01-01-001 dated 7 Dec 06.

Podsakoff, P. M., MacKenzie, S. B., Moorman, R. H., & Fetter, R. (1990). Transformational leader behaviours and their effects on followers trust in leader, satisfaction, organizational citizenship behaviours. *Leadership Quarterly, 1*, 107-142.

Quiñones, M. A. (1995). Pre-training context effects: training assignment as feedback. *Journal of Applied Psychology, 80 (2)*, 226–238.

Reiss, K. (2007). *Leadership and coaching for educators*. Thousand Oaks, CA: Corwin Press.

Rokeach, M. (1973). *The Nature of human Values*. New York: Free Press.

Scandura, T, A., & Schriesheim, C, A. (1994). Leader–member exchange and supervisor career mentoring as complementary constructs in leadership research. *Academy of Management Journal, 37*, 1588–1602.

Schwartz, S, H. (1992). Universals in the content and structure of values: Theoretical advances and empirical tests in 20 countries. *Advances in Experimental Social Psychology, 25*, 1-65.

Shamir, B., & Howell, J, M. (1999). Organizational and contextual influences on the emergence and effectiveness of charismatic leadership. *The Leadership Quarterly, 10*, 257-283.

Sosik, J, J., Godshalk, V, M., & Yammarino, F, J. (2004). Transformational leadership, learning goal orientation, and expectations for career success in mentor-protégé relationships: A multiple levels of analysis perspective. *The leadership Quarterly 15*, 241-261.

Sosik, J, J., Avolio. B, J., & Kahai, S, S. (1997). Effects of leadership style and anonymity on group potency and effectiveness in a group decision support system environment. *Journal of Applied Psychology, 82*: 89-103.

Thorndike, Edward (1932), *The Fundamentals of Learning*, AMS Press Inc.

Van Hoose, D. (1999). Army civilian leadership training — past, present and future. *Military Review, 79 (3)*, 42–47.

Whitmore, J. (2003). *Coaching for Performance*. Nicholas Brealey Publishing.

M A. Grant

Abbreviations

APEL – Approved Prior Education Learning.

ASLS – ARTD Staff Leadership School.

BD – Business Development.

CEO – Chief Executive Officer.

C&G – City & Guilds.

COO – Chief Operating Officer.

COE – Contemporary Operating Environment.

DCTS – Defence Centre of Training Support.

DIFD – Department for International Development.

DTLI – Differential Transformational Leadership Inventory.

DTTT – Defence Train the Trainer.

EQ – Emotional Quotient.

GROW – Goal, Reality, Options and Will.

HCDC - House of Commons Defence Committee.

HR – Human Resources.

ILM – Institute for Leadership and Management.

IQ – Intelligence Quotient.

KPA – Key Performance Area

KPIs – Key Performance Indicators.

MC – Master Coach.

ROI – Return On Investment.

SME – Subject Matter Expert.

STD - Self Determination Theory.

SUC – Sub Unit Coach.

TLB – Transformational Leadership Behaviour.

TO – Training Officer.

TTT – Train the Trainer.

VBL – Values Based Leadership.

UAE – United Arab Emirates.

UK – United Kingdom.

M A. Grant

ABOUT THE AUTHOR

M A. Grant is a dedicated and motivated values driven individual, he has mentored leaders and supported organizations as they shape and develop their leadership styles and cultural identities.

He has more than twenty years strategic, advisory and operational experience in the fields of leadership, management and corporate innovation. This has stretched across a wide range of international governmental and private sector organizations.

He has a genuine interest in personnel development and the growth of human capital with a proven ability to unleash people's real potential.

.

www.ingramcontent.com/pod-product-compliance
Lightning Source LLC
Chambersburg PA
CBHW070857180526
45168CB00005B/1855